Twayne's English Authors Series

Sylvia E. Bowman, *Editor*

INDIANA UNIVERSITY

William Golding

TEAS 57

William Golding

By BERNARD F. DICK
Iona College

Twayne Publishers, Inc.   ::   New York

Library of Congress Catalog Card Number: 67–19351

For ANITA and KATHERINE

Preface

William Golding is an anomaly—a former schoolmaster with a passion for Greek literature and boating, a novelist who owes nothing to his contemporaries and can easily bypass a London literary party. He possesses and cultivates every quality that would ordinarily militate against a successful career in the arts. Despite his small body of writing, Golding has been hailed as the dean of his generation of novelists, damned as a poseur who confuses gimmick with dénouement, and criticized as a faulty stylist. His first novel, *Lord of the Flies,* finally appeared in 1954 after being rejected by twenty-one publishers; the author was then forty-three, not exactly the most auspicious age for beginning a literary career. By 1962, when Golding had three other novels to his credit, *Lord of the Flies* was a campus best-seller and required reading in countless "Introduction to Literature" courses. Yet many teachers, after they had analyzed the life force out of the novel, concluded that it was pretentious, "easy," and "fool's gold."

Since Golding has suffered as much from his admirers as from his detractors, the present study is an attempt to steer a mid-course between eulogy and invective. Extremism can be avoided if the *corpus* itself is the focus of attention, plus influences which the author himself admits or which were part of his educational heritage. Sigmund Freud, Franz Kafka, Jean-Paul Sartre, and even Joseph Conrad are absent from the Golding bookcase; a Freudian reading of *Lord of the Flies* or an Existentialist interpretation of *Free Fall* may establish interesting parallels with these writers but yield nothing conclusive. In fact, the Golding novels suffer in the comparison since their structure is much simpler and on the surface less impressive than the works of these famous authors.

Golding has, however, read Ballantyne, H. G. Wells, and Euripides; and, while he admits an indebtedness to them, he still vigorously maintains that "one book does not come out of another unless it is stillborn." Yet, if Golding occupies a room in Henry James's House of Fiction, the portal through which he views reality looks back to the past rather than out at the present—back to the timeless world of the Greeks. He has constantly stressed his Hellenic parentage, claiming Homer, Herodotus, Aeschylus, Sophocles, and Euripides as kinsmen. It is impossible to separate the spirit of Greek tragedy from *Lord of the Flies* or from *The Spire,* for it must enter into a discussion of at least these two novels. Although one may try to follow Golding's dictum and not tamper with a book's genesis, every form of life, fictional or otherwise, takes on its fullest meaning when placed in its proper genealogical perspective. Even Golding must admit that the parts are intelligible only in terms of the whole.

The present study is an attempt to trace Golding's growth as a writer from his undergraduate poetry to his most mature novel, *The Spire.* Golding has also written a number of essays which throw considerable light on his technique as a novelist and also on recurrent themes in his fiction. These essays will be used in two ways: first, as part of the discussion of the novels which they elucidate; secondly, as epigraphs for various chapters.

Since so much has been written on Golding's debt to other writers, this study will include only the influences which the author himself admits or which figured prominently in his education. Many teachers find it useful to discuss Sigmund Freud and Sir James G. Frazer in connection with *Lord of the Flies,* but Golding acknowledges allegiance to neither. In fact, Golding has warned interviewers on several occasions that he owes little to contemporary literature; and in fairness to him, the warning should be heeded.

For permission to quote I would like to acknowledge Coward-McCann, Inc., for *Lord of the Flies* and *Pincher Martin;* and

Preface

Harcourt, Brace & World, Inc., for *The Inheritors, Free Fall* and *The Spire*. I would also like to thank the following: Martin Esslin and George MacBeth of The British Broadcasting Corporation in London for making available to me two of Golding's unpublished radio plays, *Break My Heart* and *Miss Pulkinhorn;* former students at Iona College who gave me the opportunity to clarify some of this material in my own mind by lecturing on it; Mr. Howard Greig of *Holiday* magazine for some valuable information about Golding's American lecture tour; and finally Mr. Golding himself, who faithfully replied to my letters and personally answered my questions on a memorable June day in Salisbury. Any study of an author is valuable only if it illuminates his intentions and lays bare the nerves of his art. Criticism is a difficult task, particularly when the subject is living. Vivisection is always more precarious than autopsy.

BERNARD F. DICK

Bronx, New York

Contents

Chronology

1911   William Golding born September 19, Cornwall, England; son of Alec Golding, Senior Master of Marlborough Grammar School, and Mildred Golding, an active worker for women's suffrage.

1930   Entered Brasenose College, Oxford, where he spent more than two years studying science, and then switched to literature.

1934   *Poems,* his first published work.

1935   Bachelor of Arts (Oxon.).

1935–   "Wasted the next four years" (by his own admission)
1939   writing, acting, and producing for a small non-West End London theater.

1939   Married Ann Brookfield and accepted position at Bishop Wordsworth's School in Salisbury.

1940   Enlisted in Royal Navy where he spent the next five years.

1945   Returned to Bishop Wordsworth's School.

1954   *Lord of the Flies.* Published in America the following year.

1955   *The Inheritors.* Published in America in 1962.

1956   *Pincher Martin.* Published in America as *The Two Deaths of Christopher Martin* (1957).

1958   *The Brass Butterfly* first performed in Oxford under the direction of Alastair Sim, who played the Emperor in this and in the London production.

1959   *Free Fall.* American edition the following year.

1960–   Book reviewer for *The Spectator.*
1962

1961   Master of Arts (Oxon.). Leaves teaching post to devote full
        time to writing.
1961–   Writer-in-residence, Hollins College, Virginia. College lec-
1962   ture tour.
1964   *The Spire.*
1965   *The Hot Gates.* Published in America the following year.

CHAPTER 1

The Thorns of Life

At noon the drowsy sun-winds brush
A shadow from the swarted corn,
At noon the linnet and the thrush
Sing dirges for the light of morn,
And oh! I think our world is dead
So much is fallen, so much is fled.
—WILLIAM GOLDING, "Song of Summer"

THE perverseness of memory and the shortage of suitable dissertation topics will never allow an author's literary *faux pas* to lie submerged in the Waters of Forgetfulness. Until his death William Faulkner lived under the black shadow of his early poetry (which was not that bad). When students at the University of Virginia confronted him with his volume *A Green Bough,* he would become apologetic and reply that the poems belonged to the twilight of adolescence but that, after realizing his limitations as a poet, he had turned to prose, "the next best thing." [1] Poetry was also William Golding's first medium, and in 1934 his collegiate views on unrequited love, the call of the sea, and the seductions of rationalism were published as part of "Macmillan's Contemporary Poets" series. Golding, as uncomfortable as Faulkner about this specter of his past, dismisses his *Poems* with an upward turn of the wrist that disclaims all responsibility for them. He also entered the world of prose—reluctantly, one suspects—for there was a nostalgic quiver in his voice when he confided, "You might say I write prose because I can't write poetry." [2]

It is not uncommon for an author to recall his apprentice work with a certain amount of disbelief, and Golding is no exception.

Yet one should remember that these twenty-nine poems were, after all, undergraduate productions; they were no better and no worse than the yearly heartbursts of the sensitive English major. As literature, they have no great value; but, as documents illustrating the young Golding's major concerns, they throw some light on an early preoccupation with two themes that later become dominant motifs in his fiction: the divided society and single-minded rationalism.

In a sonnet entitled "Non-Philosopher's Song" (a title that wonderfully illustrates the typical collegiate mistaking of rebellion for irony), he shows a definite but not unusual awareness of a dichotomy between heart and head: "Love and Reason live apart/In separate cells of head and heart." In the novels there is always the dichotomy of two worlds and the polarization of two wisdoms. But in the sonnet, the poet's lady, like the Dantesque *donna*, links the two worlds: "But oh! my lady, she and I,/We give philosophy the lie." To the young Golding, love is the bridge, a statement at once deceptively simple and paradoxically profound. And yet the poet is correct: love indeed conquers and, one might add, bridges all. But the Golding who enlisted in the Royal Navy in 1940 and witnessed the D-Day invasion of Normandy was unable to recapture the optimism of his Oxford days. "There is no bridge," declares Sammy Mountjoy, the author's *persona*, in *Free Fall*.

Golding has always objected to a catechetical view of the universe and to the reduction of human behavior to equations. The rationalist, a familiar Golding character whose mind has developed at the expense of his emotions, assumes various guises—Piggy in *Lord of the Flies*, Nick Shales in *Free Fall*, Phanocles in *The Brass Butterfly*. But he is always the oversimplifier who tries to tidy up the human heart that is too often *en déshabillé*, the pragmatist who sees only surfaces and never the dark recesses that cry for illumination.

Golding was an anti-rationalist even in his youth; his poem, "Mr. Pope," the most significant one in the collection, is an attack on devotion to the rationally conceived ideal with the Neoclassical poet as target. Again the student-poet soars on the wings of Shelley's skylark but grows short of breath while scaling Pope's "giddy heights" of creation. What is so refreshing about "Mr. Pope" is the wit, however incipient, that informs the poem and keeps it from degenerating into invective, although one suspects that the young Golding thought he was being thoroughly devastating:

> Mr. Pope walked in the park—
> Trim rows of flowers
> Embroider'd the well-order'd dark
> Where marched the marshalled hours.
>
> The trees stood silent, two by two
> Pagodas lifted up their heads
> From neatly weeded laurel-groves
> And well-spaced flower-beds.
>
> Then down a quiet gravel path—
> For Mr. Pope eschewed the sod—
> The gentleman pursued his way
> To raise his hat to Mr. God.
>
> "Dear Sir," he said, "I must confess
> This is a chastely ordered land,
> But one thing mars its loveliness,
> The stars are rather out of hand"—
>
> "If they would dance a minuet
> Instead of roaming wild and free
> Or stand in rows all trim and neat
> How exquisite the sky would be!"

Golding never lost his suspicion of a discipline that only develops one aspect of man, whether it be Neoclassicism or a science that shuns the eternal for the temporal. He still chides "those who think they have an easy answer to all problems simply because they have never looked further than the rash appearing on the skin." [3]

CHAPTER 2

The Anarchy Within

"If there is any boy or man who loves to be melancholy and morose, and who cannot enter with kindly sympathy into the regions of fun, let me seriously advise him to shut my book and put it away. It was not meant for him."

Ralph Rover
—R. M. BALLANTYNE, Preface to *The Coral Island*

"I think [*Lord of the Flies*] is in fact a *realistic* view of the Ballantyne situation."

—WILLIAM GOLDING, "The Meaning of It All"

TWENTY years elapsed before Golding published again, but he was not entirely idle during those two decades. There was, first of all, World War II which completely shattered his Candide-like optimism: "When I was young, before the war, I did have some airy-fairy views about man. . . . But I went through the war and that changed me. The war taught me different and a lot of others like me." [1] Secondly, Golding read Greek assiduously "not because it was the snobbish thing to do or even the most enjoyable, but because this is where the meat is," [2] wrote four novels that never saw publication, and engaged in literary parodies at which he could later look back in amusement.

Significantly, his first published novel, *Lord of the Flies* (1954), is something of a parody, but not in the sense of a lampoon or travesty, for Golding does not attach anything pejorative to the word. To him, parody "is subtly rooted in admiration." [3] By parody Golding means something very close to T. S. Eliot's "mature" borrowing—the transforming of the work of predecessors into something that is at once traditional and novel. But parody, if it is to be successful, must also be critical. Virgil's *Aeneid* has been called a "serious parody" of Homer, not in the sense that the Roman poet intended to spoof the *Iliad* and the *Odyssey*, but rather to transform them into something more meaningful to his age. For example, death is a common occurrence in Homer, and the battle scenes in the *Iliad* are often merely gruesome without any human significance, but Virgil, who uses Homer's battle descriptions, transforms them into an indictment of war itself. This is the poet's way of saying that, to a "modern" of the first century B.C., war is more than a series of conventional descriptions or formulae of oral epic.

As a result of his reading in Greek, Golding was steeped in a literature in which originality consisted of uniting "tradition and the individual talent." His first novel is, in many respects, an outgrowth of his literary heritage—a parody in his own sense of the term. Thus, there is nothing startlingly original about the "marooned boys" theme of *Lord of the Flies;* one may legitimately claim that the very same situation is found in science fiction or in "survival literature" and that the ideology is oddly redolent of Greek tragedy. Golding would heartily concur, for *Lord of the Flies* is a reworking of a boyhood favorite, Robert Michael Ballantyne's *The Coral Island.* And Golding's book was written from the standpoint of a man who saw his youthful illusions shattered by a world war and then withdrew into Greek literature "where the meat is." [4]

I *Barefoot Boys*

In 1857 Ballantyne published *The Coral Island,* [5] something of a children's classic in England, in which three boys are shipwrecked on an unidentified Pacific island—Ralph Rover, the fifteen-year-old narrator; Jack Martin, "a tall, strapping broad-shouldered youth of eighteen, with a handsome, good-humoured, firm face"; and Peterkin Gay, "little, quick, funny, decidedly mischievous, and about fourteen years old" (16). The lads live in "uninterrupted harmony and happiness" (220), presumably without the aftereffects of original sin, although faint, postlapsarian rumblings can be heard in some of their activities, and especially in Peterkin's butchery of an old sow to get leather for "future" shoes. But these intimations of mortality are always muted since Victorian schoolboys do not kill for pleasure. Cannibals are also encountered, but one can overlook heathen bloodletting. At the end of the novel, just when the boys think they will be devoured by savages, they are released into the hands of their *deus ex machina* teacher who announces that " 'through the great goodness of God you are free!' " (429). The natives have embraced Christianity, and Dr. Pangloss has triumphed after all.

To a generation that has witnessed two world wars, Ballantyne's simplistic psychology can only be regarded with a cynical smirk. One is almost tempted to mimick Brack's feeble reaction to Hedda Gabler's suicide (" 'People don't do things like that' ") and to consign *The Coral Island* to the bedtime reading of the very young, the very old, or historians of ideas.

In *Lord of the Flies*, Golding scrutinizes the Ballantyne premise with eyes that bequeath a legacy of experience:

You see, really, I'm getting at myself in this [novel]. What I'm saying to myself is, "Don't be such a fool, you remember when you were a boy, a small boy, how you lived on that island with Ralph and Jack and Peterkin" (who is Simon, by the way, Simon called Peter, you see. It was worked out very carefully in every possible way, this novel). I said to myself finally, "Now you are grown up, you are adult; it's taken you a long time to become adult, but now you've got there you can see that people are not like that; they would not behave like that if they were God-fearing English gentlemen, and they went to an island like that." [6]

Golding's protagonists are also named Ralph and Jack, but the character of Peterkin is split into Piggy and Simon. Along with an indeterminate number of other boys ranging in age from six to twelve, they are also abandoned on a South Sea island, presumably after being evacuated from Britain during an atomic war. Like the Ballantyne trio, they also hunt pigs; but none of the Victorian lads would ever have sodomized the animal with a spear, since sexual defacement is apparently a vice known only to our era. But there is no "uninterrupted harmony and happiness" on this island, and the rules which Ralph thought would transform the motley group into a junior Utopia are irrevocably broken when the desire to hunt supersedes the more utilitarian needs for a continually burning fire, shelter, and sanitation. The hunters don war paint and kill off or absorb any parliamentarians, except Ralph, who refuses to revert to savagery and who is left to be smoked out of his hiding place and hunted down. The fire that envelops the island is spotted by a navy cruiser, and Ralph and the remnants of the group are rescued after having received the best possible initiation into adulthood.

Lord of the Flies introduces a structural principle that becomes Golding's hallmark: a polarity expressed in terms of a moral tension. Thus, there is the rational (the fire-watchers) pitted against the irrational (the hunters) in *Lord of the Flies;* Neanderthal man absorbed by the fitter species of Homo sapiens (*The Inheritors*); fallen man confronting God (*Pincher Martin*); science and humanism (*Free Fall*); and the vision versus the reality (*The Spire*). Consequently, a Golding novel is reminiscent of a skeletal framework that is deliberately and at times deceptively simple.

Golding starts from what might be called "the island premise." All "island literature" is essentially similar: castaways can live either in harmony or in anarchy. Every dramatic situation is potentially tragic or comic, depending upon the author's purpose. The "abandoned child" theme can produce Sophocles' *Oedipus the King* or Oscar Wilde's *The Importance of Being Earnest,* each of which is a valid artistic elaboration of an archetypal motif. Since there is tragic potential in the comic, and seeds of comedy in the tragic, the author's vision alone differentiates between them and creates the path which his plot takes. Golding has chosen chaos instead of order. Although the "island premise" admits of three possibilities for characterization—children (*The Coral Island*), adults (*Robinson Crusoe*), or a combination (*The Swiss Family Robinson*)—Golding has selected the first. Some explanation must be given for the absence of adults, and it is immediately supplied: " 'He [the pilot] must have flown off after he dropped us' " (12).[7] Thus far, there is nothing unique about Golding's development of the premise, except for the peculiarly modern use of an atomic holocaust to account for the evacuation.

The next events follow directly from the island premise. Piggy discovers a seashell ("the conch") which soon becomes a symbol of authority, and Ralph uses it to call together the dispersed community. The boys gradually assemble from various parts of the island, and something akin to a Homeric assembly takes place in which Ralph plays Agamemnon and Piggy, a sagacious Nestor, bustles about soliciting names. Presentiments of demoralization soon occur when Ralph sees "something dark . . . fumbling along" (26). The amorphous blackness then becomes a "creature" and finally identifies itself as a group of black-clad choir boys led by Jack Merridew, who immediately wants to be elected chief of the community because he is chapter chorister and can sing C sharp. Ralph wins the election, and the society splits into two halves: the firewatchers and the choir turned hunters.

The chaotic rumblings grow in intensity until at the end of the chapter Jack spots a pig, but is unable to kill it. "Next time there would be no mercy" (41). From this point on, the plot can take only one course. Golding has already superimposed his vision on *The Coral Island* and the lines zigzag, refusing to coincide with Ballantyne's optimistic cartography.

The polarity from which Golding is working first isolates itself in two sets of characters—Ralph and Jack, Piggy and Simon. Ralph is fair-haired, "but there was a mildness about his mouth and eyes that proclaimed no devil" (15). Jack, on the other hand, is red-haired, a Satanic figure dressed in black: "His face was crumpled and freckled, and ugly without silliness. Out of this face stared two light blue eyes, frustrated now, and turning, or ready to turn, to anger" (27); he is hardly the "handsome, good-humoured" lad he was in his Victorian incarnation. A tension stemming from the opposite natures of Ralph and Jack is immediately established; it is all the more pathetic because neither boy understands the unspoken animosity that exists between them. At the end of Chapter One, when the pig is seen, Golding catches this smouldering resentment in a fragment of dialogue in which each discharges his words like a volley:

"You should stick a pig," said Ralph fiercely.
"They always talk about sticking a pig."
"You cut a pig's throat to let the blood out," said Jack, "otherwise you can't eat the meat."
"Why didn't you—?" (41).

When Jack strikes his blade into a tree trunk, the next best substitute for the pig, his action can only presage ill.

Just as Ralph and Jack are opposites, and as such are painted in monochrome, so, too, are Piggy and Simon. Piggy, the fat, near-sighted asthmatic, is an incipient rationalist and functions as Ralph's prime minister. It is Piggy who teaches the theory-prone Ralph how to use the conch; because Piggy is short-winded, he cannot blow into it himself. Endowed with a maturity that is at times precocity, he has quite early in life found his answers in science and in a prissy rationalism. " 'Like kids!' " (50) is his indictment of the antics of the "littluns." He alone wears glasses, a symbol of political vision, which act, while they remain intact, as a sort of "mirror for magistrates."

Simon, one of the choristers, is first seen recovering from a fainting spell. He has been blessed and cursed with the gift of prophecy but, like Cassandra, is doomed to be ignored. Since he is an epileptic (or so his fainting spells seem to indicate), his clairvoyance is a compensation for his physical suffering. Simon alone knows that the reason for the dissolution of the community lies in man's devil-ridden nature, but he cannot communicate his understanding to the others.

For the island society to function harmoniously, each group should complement the other. Ralph and Jack, who represent extremes of the politician and the warrior, respectively, require the tempering influence of an astute prime minister who is not a born leader and of a high priest whose clairvoyance is born of the pain of knowledge. Ralph's theoretical knowledge requires Piggy's practicality. As an inarticulate seer, Simon inhabits the world of the irrational—Jack's world; and, since both were choir boys, they should share the sudden camaraderie that grows out of choral worship. If Golding were a medieval hagiographer, one ray from Simon's halo would transform Jack's obsession with hunting into a spiritual good. But Golding will not concede to apocrypha, and his Coral Island is not divided into various classes that cooperate for coexistence. Instead, each character goes his own way along with what he symbolizes, unheeded by the other. Piggy realizes Ralph's limitations as a leader and votes for him with reluctance. Jack and his choristers smear their bodies with paint, leaving the fire to burn itself out. Ralph is preoccupied with shelter and sanitation, and Simon withdraws to a secluded part of the island inhabited only by butterflies.[8]

The Utopian ideal should be realizable in a community of children since they are freer from the prejudices and class distinctions that come with maturity. The child can supply inaccurate but spontaneous answers to everything; his mind is untainted by the scholastic syllogism. One would like to believe all of this, but it is only partially true. If the child is the father of man, then as a future parent he also has the potency for adult evil. The only difference is that with children there will be sporadic eruptions of violence rather than cunning machinations because there is no sophisticated dialectic, no diabolical subtlety engineering the process.

The inevitable anarchy that sweeps the island stems from the children's inability to disentangle cause and effect. It is not until the end of the novel that Ralph experiences one blinding moment of tragic perception that destroys his youthful illusions. At the beginning, he can only say, " 'It's a good island' " (45). One can almost hear Pope's soothing refrain, "All partial evil, universal good," echoing through Ralph's naïveté. But the others behave "as if it wasn't a good island." When the pillars of society completely give way, Ralph can only cry helplessly.

[24]

Ralph's devotion to parliamentary procedure adumbrates his relationship with Jack, and Golding admirably shows how their antagonism developed from conflicting ideologies. Ralph's attitude toward Piggy and Simon is at best one of passive toleration: he finds Piggy a bore; and, when he smiles at his prime minister, his smile is interpreted as a token of friendship when it is really a smirk that one might give an underling whose bustling activities are so much wasted energy. His relationship with Simon is less well defined because he regards Simon's insights as dark allusions. When Simon prophesies that he will finally be rescued, Ralph smiles again, but his is the radiance of someone whose spirits have suddenly been buoyed up. He exchanges no smiles with Jack, because his commitment to reason and order completely shuts out the world of the hunter. In an episode that is curiously moving in a detached way, Jack tries to explain the irrational urges that come over him while hunting—the first and only time that he tries to win Ralph's acceptance of his way of life:

Jack leapt to his feet and spoke very quickly. "That's how you can feel in the forest. Of course there's nothing in it. Only—only—" He took a few rapid steps towards the beach, then came back.
"Only I know how they feel. See? That's all."
"The best thing we can do is get ourselves rescued."
Jack had to think for a moment before he could remember what rescue was.
"Rescue? Yes, of course! All the same, I'd like to catch a pig first—" He snatched up his spear and dashed it into the ground. The opaque, mad look came into his eyes again.
Ralph looked at him critically through his tangle of fair hair.
"So long as your hunters remember the fire—"
"You and your fire!" (67–68).

Jack turns to Ralph, the humanist who has no patience with incoherence; and the scene ends with two lines of dialogue and two self-assertive voices speaking at opposite ends of a Tower of Babel:

[25]

"If I could only get a pig!"
"I'll come back and go on with the shelter" (70).

One thinks of John Steinbeck's *Of Mice and Men,* where Lennie and Curley's wife talk entirely at cross-purposes, each expressing his selfhood without paying any heed to the other. Like Steinbeck's characters, Ralph and Jack speak without cues since theirs is a debate without possibility of rebuttal.

II *Symbol and Irony*

Although Golding is working from the "island premise," he is not merely weaving a tangled skein of episodes. Complementing the literal action is a moral or symbolic one that is, for the most part, an unspoken commentary on the episodes; and each significant act has a corresponding symbolism. The conch represents order, and its possession entitles the holder to free speech in the assembly. The fire denotes the spirit of civilization which must be continually fed. It acquires further symbolism if one recalls the torchlight race at the opening of Plato's *Republic* where riders on horseback pass flaming torches back and forth, showing that athletic perseverance is necessary for the unbroken transmission of culture.

Golding relies heavily on the use of irony to underscore the symbolic action. The fire that was made by the reflection of light from Piggy's glasses goes out when Jack kills his first pig. The smashing of one of the lenses throws the community into semi-barbarism, and the anti-Promethean theft of the other leads to a complete reversion to savagery. With the loss of his glasses, the rational Piggy is reduced to strident hysteria. When Ralph prays for a sign from heaven, his prayer is returned in the form of a dead paratrooper who bobs up and down like a macabre puppet. The children identify the corpse with a mythical beast who they believe stalks the island. A pig hunt is staged, and its ritual provides motifs for the deaths of Simon and Piggy, and the subsequent tracking down of Ralph. When Simon discovers the truth about the "beast," he tries to tell the others who are re-enacting

the hunt; but, mistaken for the beast, he is brutally murdered.
Jack's sadistic lieutenant, Roger, strikes Piggy with a stone as he
clings to the conch, now divested of its symbolism and reduced to
a meaningless seashell; Piggy plunges to his death, his limbs
twitching "like a pig's after it has been killed" (223). The hunters
outlaw Ralph and sharpen a stick at both ends, presumably to kill
and impale him like a pig. They smoke him out of hiding by a fire
that grows out of control and sweeps across the island, thereby
attracting the attention of a navy cruiser and supplying the ironi-
cal dénouement.

III   *Beelzebub, Prince of Devils*

Sooner or later, the reader must confront the meaning of the
title which, like all of Golding's symbolism, is linked with the
events of the novel. Thus, even for purposes of discussion, it cannot be isolated from the action. "Lord of the flies" is a translation
of *Beelzebub*, the Greek transliteration of the Hebrew *Ba'alzevuv*,
and in Judaism and Christianity denotes the principle of evil per-
sonified—the Devil, Satan, Mephistopheles. Golding equates the
"Lord of the Flies" with the demonic force latent in man; it is
generally kept in check by the rational part of human nature, but
in the absence of reason or social pressure, breaks out in an act of
barbaric bloodletting. This force has been called by a variety of
names, depending upon whether one is a theologian, a poet, or a
humanist: original sin, "Adam's Curse," "the darkness of man's
heart," "The Banality of Evil." To the realist the demonic is
merely a corollary of the theorem of existence; as a concomitant of
human nature, it cannot be ignored, and only the saint can sur-
mount it by asceticism.

Golding does not immediately symbolize his philosophy of evil,
but in his usual way allows it to flow from a series of events. First,
the "littluns" complain of seeing an imaginary beast; the fear that
has grown out of their fitful imaginations, which must attach itself
to an object, finds an outlet in the dead paratrooper. The hunters,
who revert to the most primitive form of expiation, transfix the
head of a slain pig on a pole as a blood offering to the "beast."

Simon comes upon the impaled head, and his confrontation with it is dramatically heralded by the disappearance of the butterflies.

The insect-covered head introduces itself as the "Lord of the Flies," an expression which, like so much in Golding, is ironically accurate. The "adult cynicism" which it imparts to Simon is significant, for the young seer has directly confronted evil without the assuring barricade of butterflies: " 'Fancy thinking the Beast was something you could hunt and kill!' said the head. For a moment or two the forest and all the other dimly appreciated places echoed with the parody of laughter. 'You knew, didn't you? I'm part of you? Close, close, close! I'm the reason why it's no go? Why things are what they are?' " (177).

Simon has communed with evil concretely embodied in a pig's head buzzing with flies, and the proximity causes him to faint. He had fainted once before when the black-robed choristers entered and cast a dark shadow on the coral island. He faints now because he has received knowledge too overwhelming to endure.

Golding's Lord of the Flies is not the biblical Satan who tempts Christ, nor the Miltonic counterpart who speaks in glorious rhetoric. Rather it is a pig's head—evil reduced to one of its vilest incarnations. Golding will have nothing to do with a suave Mephistopheles or a honey-tongued Lucifer; his Devil is more in keeping with Dorian Gray's decaying portrait because it abandons rhetorical finery for the stark reality of spiritual corruption. The Lord of the Flies was correct: the beast is in man; and, when it expresses itself, it is in the form of a rotting self-portrait.

But the Lord of the Flies is also the Lord of Dung, and there is ample reference to excrement in the novel. The island becomes dotted with feces because the "littluns" refuse to cooperate with Ralph's sanitation program. When Simon tries to convey the meaning of the "beast" to the others, he asks timidly, " 'What's the dirtiest thing there is?' " (111). Jack's response to Simon's delicately phrased question was apparently the well-known four-letter word. If Satan is the Lord of the Flies, he is also the Lord of Dung. When man serves this lord, he will wear the same emblem that characterizes his master. Thus evil is more than the rotting head of a pig: it is literally "the dirtiest thing there is," and its most graphic depiction would be the very popular Anglo-Saxon word.

IV   *Two Worlds, Two Wisdoms*

To the ancient Greeks, Dionysus was the god of animal potency, the mythological incarnation of the life principle; it was he who gave life to plant, animal, and man.[9] He inspired his votaries to wild frenzies, perhaps even human sacrifice. Dionysus symbolized the elemental in animal and human nature; as such, he cannot be ignored; for to inhibit man's inclination to emotional expression is to deny him his most natural form of worship. Dionysus can be docile when he is propitiated; but, when he is excluded by a religion of the mind, he is no longer a tame god and exacts a vengeance that exceeds human expectations. Apollo, on the other hand, represents the civilizing arts—healing, poetry, music, law and order. As god of light, he illuminates rather than beclouds the mind.

There is a marked and perennial conflict between the Dionysian and Apollonian, the rational and irrational worlds. In *The Birth of Tragedy out of the Spirit of Music*, Nietzsche puts forth his famous distinction between the two: he saw Greek art as the end result of a continual tension between them—the temperate Apollonian striving to assimilate the wild and unconscious Dionysian.

Lord of the Flies can also be read in the light of the Dionysian-Apollonian dichotomy, and this interpretation is rapidly becoming the orthodox one, especially since early in his career Golding declared his debt to Greek tragedy, specifically to Euripides.[10] In the *Bacchae*, probably his last and certainly his most difficult play, Euripides dramatizes the eternal conflict between mind and heart, reason and emotion. He shows that the way up and down is not the same, but that both paths must continually cross without superseding each other. Pentheus, the king of Thebes, is rooted in a frigid intellectualism that will not admit the irrational. Thus he refuses to acknowledge the new religion that has swept the city and has found votaries in his mother, Agave, and in Cadmus and

Teiresias, both of whom warn him that the worship of Dionysus must be given a hearing. Dionysus even assumes human form to warn Pentheus, and in a startling scene begins to take on the appearance of a bull; but Pentheus, who is blind to the animal forms in which the god was worshiped, can only gape at the metamorphosis. When Dionysus induces Pentheus to observe his worshipers, the Bacchants, he suggests that Pentheus wear women's clothes to escape detection. At the height of the ritual, the women discover him in a fir tree; and, goaded by a frenzy that makes them oblivious to moral laws, they hunt him down and dismember him. Agave appears triumphantly with her son's head on a thyrsus, still under the ecstatic spell of communion with the deity and thinking that she holds the head of a lion, one of the sacred animals of Dionysus. There is a break in the text at verse 1329, but it is clear from the plot-summary attached to certain manuscripts and from the final scene that Dionysus appeared at the end of the play as *deus ex machina* and banished Agave from her native city.

Both *Lord of the Flies* and the *Bacchae* are anthropological passion plays in which individuals—children in Golding, adults in Euripides—revert to savagery and murder during a frenzied ritual. Both portray a divided society in which the Apollonian has not fully assimilated the Dionysian. In the *Bacchae* the polarity consists in the followers of Dionysus and in Pentheus, who alone opposes the religion. Early in the novel, some of the marooned boys in whom the irrational instinct is paramount separate from the rest to become hunters; and their Dionysian character is subtly underscored by the fact that they were former choristers. The novel centers on the attempt of the hunters first to absorb, then to destroy the rational element in much the same way as Pentheus was first persuaded by Cadmus and Teiresias to join the new cult, only to reject it and be killed at the hand of the Bacchants. Furthermore, both works have *deus ex machina* endings. In the *Bacchae*, Dionysus appeared to foretell the fortunes of all. A more human epiphany occurs at the end of the novel when the naval officer comes to the rescue and resolves the action in a highly Euripidean manner. But, in view of the previous bloodshed on the island this epiphany is as ironic as the appearance of Dionysus at the close of the *Bacchae*.

Specifically, both drama and novel contain three interrelated ritual themes: the cult of a beast-god, a hunt as prefiguration of the death of the scapegoat-figure, and the dismemberment of the scapegoat. Golding deviates in only one respect from Euripides: logically Ralph, the Pentheus in embryo, should be the scapegoat; but the author assigns this role to Simon, allowing Ralph to live instead with his new-found knowledge of "the darkness of man's heart."

Euripides depicts a Dionysus who still retains his original characteristics of a beast-deity, the incarnation of animal potency with which his votaries sought communion. Dionysus is both hunter and hunted; consequently, beast-hunt imagery pervades the drama (verses 101, 137, 436, 920, 1017, 1188 ff.). But more important, the *Bacchae* is the enactment of a ritualistic sacrifice in which the victim is first made to resemble the god before he is dismembered. Thus, Pentheus, the scapegoat, is cajoled into wearing the Dionysian attire before going to observe the Bacchants. His death had been prefigured earlier in a scene in which a messenger described how the frenzied women dismembered a herd of cattle. When Pentheus is finally discovered in the fir tree, he is literally hunted down and killed.

In *Lord of the Flies*, the obsession with the hunt transforms the hunters into a nameless group that functions conjointly but without personal identity: "the throb and stamp of a single organism" (187). Their choral refrain, *"Kill the beast! Cut his throat! Spill his blood!"* suggests the "hunt, kill, prey" of the Bacchants. The killing of the sow prefigures the death of Simon, the scapegoat, in much the same way as the raid on the cattle foreshadowed that of Pentheus. The pig's head is impaled on a stick (a reminiscence of Pentheus' head on the thyrsus?), and is offered as a trophy to the imaginary beast. When Simon accidentally interrupts the re-enactment of the pig-hunt, he is mistaken for the beast and killed.

Lastly, both Pentheus and Simon are pitted against elemental forces that are their direct opposites. Pentheus alone sees Dionysus in animal shape, but he can neither recognize the god nor understand that his own intellectualism must be complemented by irrational yet necessary passions. Only Simon hears the cynical message of the Lord of the Flies, assuring the child that "everything was a bad business" (170). Confronted with the nonrational, Simon recognizes it, for it is an "ancient, inescapable recognition" (171). But such recognition brings either a loss of innocence or death, and Simon is wantonly destroyed by a surge of anarchy that is inevitable in a divided universe.

In the *Bacchae*, Euripides has dramatized the ageless dichotomy of reason and emotion; he has shown how a refusal to recognize the needs of a lower but natural consciousness brings a destruction that far exceeds the offense. Dionysus is a more primitive power than Apollo, and his revenge will be as disproportionate as his worship. Translated into modern terms, the play's theme would be that repression of the natural palliates and disembodies man, reducing him to matterless spirit and thereby antagonizing his lower self. But, at the same time, Euripides has implicitly shown how ecstatic mysticism, in itself a valid and desirable form of worship, degenerates into an orgiastic sensuality when rational limits are not imposed upon it. Both Pentheus and the Bacchants have erred in cleaving man in two and in deifying the parts and not the whole.

Golding, at least in *Lord of the Flies*, sees no resolution to the polarity. There will always be fire-watchers and hunters who will live in temporary harmony, but more often in glowering stalemates or open conflict that only a miraculous intervention can halt. Thus the arrival of the immaculately attired naval officer is a literal *deus ex machina* in the Euripidean sense: the situation has strayed beyond the boundaries of a fictional reality into an area where chance or providence reside. A fortuitous occurrence such as a fire can alone save the characters and the work. The author is helpless because the moral problem cannot be solved by a final period, the sudden conversion of the hunters à la Ballantyne, or Ralph's death. Even the *Bacchae* does not end with Pentheus' dismemberment or with Agave's realization of her deed. It must terminate with the appearance of Dionysus who alone can bring the action to a close.

Golding's ending is so constructed that it could never be interpreted as the final solution to the problem. Who will rescue the cruiser? The neatly dressed naval officer is a Dionysian; he is also "hunting." If the ending must be considered a "gimmick" (and *deus ex machina* is better),[11] then it is as valid as the one which Brecht used in *The Threepenny Opera* when the "Victorious Messenger" saves Macheath from the gallows, although the audience is warned that in real life such messengers are rare. The *ex machina* ending is necessary for Golding's purpose: knowledge must come from this suffering, if the island nightmare is to have any real value. Simon alone understood what evil was, but he could not communicate it. At the very end Ralph experiences a blinding intuition and weeps uncontrollably "for the end of innocence, the darkness of man's heart, and the fall through the air of the true, wise friend called Piggy."

What makes the *Bacchae* an overpowering tragedy and *Lord of the Flies* an engrossing exercise in melodrama is the treatment of the theme. Golding is torn between conveying a philosophy of evil and writing a realistic novel about the Dionysian-Apollonian polarity which poets like Euripides, philosophers like Nietzsche, or novelists like Dostoevski, who in a sense is both, can treat more comfortably. Golding's knowledge of children is admirable; he catches their half-formed sentences and spontaneous vulgarities, but these realistic touches are only externals since one hears them as children but sees them as adults. The situation itself is also unconvincing. Ralph describes the island as "'icing . . . on a pink cake'" (34); and, although the icing has a bitter taste, the setting never becomes anything other than its initial description. It is almost as if the children were unleashed on a Hollywood sound stage to enact their games against the frowzy backdrop of a jungle extravaganza.

V *Assessment*

What limits *Lord of the Flies* to the category of a "minor classic" and sets it apart from other novels that explore the problem of evil is precisely the use of children. Isolating the moral dichotomy in a group of boys invariably robs the work of any tragic stature it might possess. When children revert to bestiality, one can only say, "the horror, the horror." There is no catharsis because there is no poetry or tragic flaw; children are incapable of either. There is no real understanding of the evil that has erupted because children are too immature to associate cause with effect; Ralph may experience an undefined glimpse into "the darkness of man's heart" (and here again Golding is looking at Ralph as if he were an adult, giving him the tragic awareness of a hero); but, as a twelve-year-old, he cannot raise this new-found knowledge into a cosmic vision. Golding himself is not at fault here; given such a theme, one cannot imagine a better treatment. The island setting further simplifies the action, reducing it to a microcosm, or perhaps even a geocosm. The work is small-scaled in both setting and character, but it reproduces man and his world in miniature.

But these are exactly the limitations that have made the novel such a popular success, particularly among high school students and undergraduates. One student found the characters embodiments of types he had known at camp.[12] The novel will always remain an excellent introduction to serious fiction because the problem of evil has been reduced to a blackboard outline easily intelligible to those whose knowledge of man is limited by age or experience.

Despite its initial fascination, *Lord of the Flies* could not remain as Golding's supreme achievement, especially after he produced *The Inheritors* the following year. Whenever the problem of evil is fictionalized, there is the latent danger of regarding it as the only fundamental truth of existence and of considering the demonic as the only real side of man. It is true that the book is a product of the author's war experiences, but it is also true that war is only one aspect, and a dirty one at that, of the human situation.

One can say the same about the present sub-genre of film and play based on the Nazi atrocities: they can jolt the viewer into a state of emotional numbness, but whatever power and immediacy they possess ultimately dissipate because they are not telling the complete story. Moreover, vice is always easier to depict than its opposite; thus, apart from the theological difficulties in the *Paradiso,* artistically it is a more spectacular performance than the *Inferno.*

Golding is only partially out of the net that enmeshes the allegorical writer. Consequently, *Lord of the Flies,* as impressive a first novel as it is, is "no go"—to use the words of the pig's head to Simon—because evil is "no go," at least as the author has presented it. One will not deny the logic of the episodes leading up to Simon's confrontation with the Lord of the Flies: the pig hunt, the offering of the head to the mythical beast, Simon's coming upon the trophy in his special part of the island. The plotting may be transparent (Golding prides himself on having meticulously worked out the novel), but there is a hard logic behind it. One only wonders why the pig's head now takes on a satanic symbolism, except perhaps because the author needed a title or because he wanted his Christ figure to come face to face with a literal Beelzebub. Golding was clearly aiming for two levels of meaning, but he succeeds only on the literal: the symbolic level is nothing more than a repetition of the literal. The explanation which the Lord of the Flies gives for the inevitable chaos is gratuitous, since the children's capacity for evil has already been made quite evident. One may well object to a footnote leaping out of the body of the text.

In 1962 Golding delivered a lecture at the University of California at Los Angeles in which he examined the nature of "fable" and used *Lord of the Flies* to illustrate some of his points. The lecture was given on other campuses and has now been transformed into a permanent gloss on the novel.[13]

The value of artists speaking on their art is a problem for the present generation of literary critics. The lecture circuit, the writer-in-residence post, and the writers' conference have all given the novelist an open forum for disseminating his views and for interpreting his works. Does one trust the tale, not the teller; or does one believe the critic, not the writer? Much of what Golding says about the fabulist as moralist is orthodox enough, but there remains the vexing symbolism that he attaches to the dead paratrooper as history that "won't lie down." In terms of the actual novel, the paratrooper whom the boys equate with the mythical beast is a catalyst that sets off a series of events including Simon's murder. It seems that Golding is doing what he deplores in scholars who superimposed Freud and Frazer on *Lord of the Flies,* and has given an incident, really a link in a carefully forged chain, a significance that exists only in the order of intention.

CHAPTER 3

Our Ancestral Ogres

"But the grisly folk we cannot begin to understand. We cannot conceive in our different minds the strange ideas that chased one another through those queerly shaped brains. As well might we try to dream and feel as a gorilla dreams and feels."

—H. G. WELLS, "The Grisly Folk"

"I believe that man suffers from an appalling ignorance of his own nature."

—WILLIAM GOLDING, "The Writer in His Age"

IN *Lord of the Flies* (1954), Golding supplied the realist's rebuttal to the wholesome optimism of *The Coral Island;* in *The Inheritors* (1955), he continues the exploration of the end of innocence, this time of a Neanderthal family. Again, Golding is taking exception to a conventional idea—H. G. Wells's superior picture of Homo sapiens. The reader first encounters a quotation from Wells's *The Outline of History* describing man's Neanderthal ancestors; and, like the customary T. S. Eliot epigraph, the Wells quotation should be considered as the novel's point of departure:

"We know very little of the appearance of the Neanderthal man, but this . . . seems to suggest an extreme hairiness, an ugliness, or repulsive strangeness in his appearance over and above his low forehead, his beetle brows, his ape neck, and his inferior stature. . . . Says Sir Harry Johnston, in a survey of the rise of modern man in his *Views and Reviews:* 'The dim racial remembrance of such gorilla-like monsters, with cunning brains, shambling gait, hairy bodies, strong teeth, and possibly cannibalistic tendencies, may be the germ of the ogre in folklore. . . .'" [1]

Golding, who was raised on Wells's *Outline,* severs the silver cord with an angry chisel:

Wells' *Outline of History* played a great part in my life because my father was a rationalist, and the *Outline* . . . was something he took neat. Well now, Wells' *Outline of History* is the rationalist's gospel *in excelsis,* I should think. I got this from my father, and by and by it seemed to me not to be large enough. It seemed to me to be too neat and slick. And when I re-read it as an adult I came across his picture of Neanderthal man, our immediate predecessors, as being the gross brutal creatures who were possibly the basis of the mythological bad man, whatever he may be, the ogre. I thought to myself that this is just absurd. What we're doing is externalising our inside.[2]

Twenty years after the *Outline,* Wells predicted *The Fate of Homo Sapiens,* which carried the clarion warning to subsequent generations of "adapt or perish." Education was the only answer for modern man. The Neanderthals, "low-browed and brutish" creatures whose skull imprisoned their brain, were fated to inhabit a culturally vacuous society bereft of creative thought. But Homo sapiens, the "true" man, the teachable animal, could train his intellect for good; it was his sworn duty, in fact, to do so.

But to this hope, Golding says no. Homo sapiens, while educable, has some dirt-streaked pages in his biography. One's belief in the inherent goodness of human nature may be buoyed up by the birth of a creative Dante or Shakespeare, but there are also Hitlers and to Golding the concentration camps were another lurid chapter in a highly censurable history. Nor will education transfigure man, as the cultivated Dr. Halde, the Nazi psychologist of *Free Fall,* proves. The specters of evil do not lie hidden in the nodes of the evolutionary chain; they dwell in "the darkness of man's heart."

Although *The Inheritors* is essentially anti-rationalist, it is not doctrinaire. The epigraph is only a *terminus a quo,* and it would even be possible to view the novel as a mythic counterpart to the fall of man and the loss of Eden. Again, Golding only supplies the skeletal outline of his theme, but what invariably happens to most works of this type is that, the simpler the lines of construction, the greater the symbolic potential of the edifice.

In any era *The Inheritors* would be a tour de force, for Golding has not only taken a type that would be repellent to readers conditioned by the bugaboos of rationalism, but has also succeeded in sympathetically re-creating a lost society complete with language patterns that vividly capture the aconceptual nature of the Neanderthal. He thinks in pictures ("'I have a picture.'"), a fact which may seem obvious enough in the light of the Wellsian description. But, when the expression is continually repeated and the pictures elaborated, one sees that these people possess something that is equally as precious as an intellect—a childlike wonder and imagination, or to use Golding's favorite word, "innocence."

Golding's Neanderthal family, apparently the last of an extinct species, consists of eight members who are introduced as they migrate from winter to summer camping grounds. Although "the people," as they are called, function as a closely knit group, their relationships within the family are at first difficult to ascertain. A similar situation was seen in *Lord of the Flies:* the boys were simply introduced as they appeared. This technique has prompted one critic to observe that "sometimes the reader himself does not know what is going on." [3] It is true that nothing like a genealogy is ever given, although the author is specifically concentrating on a family, and that Golding does not introduce characters with anything resembling social formality; he does not wish to create a network of characters à la Iris Murdoch. Since the characters are ultimately subordinate to the situation (or the myth) out of which their relationships with one another grow, the reader who wishes a web of connections among members of the family will be at a loss. One can at best speak of the characters in generalizations: there is the dying patriarch, Mal; his wife, "the old woman"; Ha and Fa, apparently mates; Nil and her baby boy, "the new one"; Lok, who also possessed Fa as a mate; and Liku, a young girl, who carries a doll-like replica of their mother goddess, Oa.

Golding demands much of the reader, and nowhere is this more obvious than in the opening pages. The reader first sees Lok, who evolves into the protagonist and finally the tragic figure, carrying Liku on his shoulders in what is apparently the Neanderthal equivalent of "piggy back." Liku is carrying "the little Oa" in such a way that it is under Lok's chin. One is immediately tempted to regard the little Oa as an infant and to wonder if the author is not straining credulity by having a trio engage in such a romp. Other references are made to the little Oa; Liku will put its head to her mouth, and at another time "the little Oa lay uncomfortably under her arm" (24).[4] The figure is also waved when the Neanderthals see an ice formation that is apparently a natural evocation of their goddess. However, the little Oa is later fed meat, but it must be remembered that Liku is speaking here: " 'I ate meat. And little Oa ate meat' " (58). Actually, the little Oa is a doll; and a child can, and does, speak of feeding her doll. In a work so economically constructed, the author can demand a close reading of the text. Golding does precisely this; he does not deceive, but on the other hand he does not pander.

The difficulties continue even after the introduction of Lok and Liku. A cursory reading leaves one with the impression that nothing of significance is happening, but this is not really true. Since Golding has dispensed with the conventional means of introduction, he begins his story in the middle in the manner of the epic. The characters are presented by their reactions to the disappearance of the log by which they had always crossed the stream. Lok responds to the loss with the eyes of one emerging from sleep; Fa, who is carrying her baby, is suspicious and at first believes that Lok planned the loss as a joke; Liku is only interested in playing; Ha, the more intelligent one, appears on the scene, as do the distraught Nil, Mal, and the old woman. The disappearance of the log is transformed into a meaningful situation that occasions the gathering of the clan, each of whom reacts differently.

The sympathy which Golding manages to evoke through the log episode is extended to embrace the plight of the family. An author so convinced of the cosmic validity of his theme is often tempted to let a wail issue through the aperture of his *persona*.

There are a few occasions in *The Inheritors* when the heart of the
prose gives every indication of breaking into a bittersweet Vien-
nese refrain that presages the end of an era, but Golding's art rests
so firmly on its lapidary construction that the lament is never
heard. In one of the finest passages of contemporary writing, he
enters the shadowy world of the Neanderthal mind, one only
slightly illuminated by the fire of Plato's cave:

One of the deep silences fell on them, that seemed so much more natural than speech, a timeless silence in which there were at first many
minds in the overhang; and then perhaps no mind at all. So fully dis-
counted was the roar of the water that the soft touch of the wind on
the rocks became audible. Their ears as if endowed with separate life
sorted the tangle of tiny sounds and accepted them, the sound of
breathing, the sound of wet clay flaking and ashes falling in (34).

The description—sympathetic, but not sentimental—glows like
Pater's "hard, gemlike flame."

The mores of the family are also delineated with compassion,
but again Golding is not delivering a panegyric on Neanderthal
integrity. He lets the tribe reveal itself by its actions which are
always characterized by a total lack of guile. "The people" only
eat meat when the animal has already been killed. Thus they can
justify their eating of a slain doe: " 'there is no blame' " (54); that
is, there has been no willful destruction of life. Their sexual
habits, while polygamous, are highly restrained. " 'We shall find
food . . . and we shall make love' " (26), says Lok. As prelapsar-
ians who are uninhibited about their nakedness, they can view
one another as people whose biological differences are merely as-
sumed but never elaborated.

Their harmony is equally endearing. When one "has a picture,"
the others listen with close attention, each attempting to help the
other out should his pictures fail, each reacting with attentiveness.
When Lok engages in buffoonery to amuse them, the members of
the family laugh with him and applaud his antics; they know his
limitations (" 'Lok has a mouthful of words and no pictures' ")
and willingly give him the limelight he requires.

But every Eden has its metaphorical apple and serpent, and is doomed to be short lived. Enveloping shadows soon begin to fall on the serene community, and the invasion of Homo sapiens is anticipated by an evening scene that is haunted by forebodings. Although the family sleeps, Lok is restless. While he tries to sleep, "there were eyes watching him from the cliffs . . ." (41). He sniffs at unfamiliar odors, but the scent eludes him. The episode reaches a descriptive and emotional climax with the appearance of a moon that rises slowly amid fragments of cloud:

The moon rose slowly and almost vertically into a sky where there was nothing but a few spilled traces of cloud. The light crawled down the island and made the pillars of spray full of brightness. It was watched by green eyes, it discovered grey forms that slid and twisted from light to shadow or ran swiftly across the open spaces on the sides of the mountain. It fell on the trees of the forest so that a scatter of faint ivory patches moved over the rotting leaves and earth. It lay on the river and the wavering weed-tails; and the water was full of tinsel loops and circles and eddies of liquid cold fire (43).

The presentiments soon become reality. Ha disappears while gathering wood with Nil; he was last seen smiling at someone on the cliff. Mal, who had grown progressively ill, dies and is buried with a simple ritual carried out with an acceptance of death as the natural concomitance of life. Soon the new people "without pictures in their heads" (103) make their appearance. One of them abducts Liku; when Lok tries to rescue her, the invader shoots a poisoned arrow at him.

Again the understatement is admirable, for Golding describes the shooting of the arrow without resorting to any prosaic statement. To Lok, who has no powers of abstraction, the arrow resembles the closest thing in nature with which he is familiar—a twig. And this is precisely how Golding describes it, always from Lok's point of view. He then smells it, and lacking a word for poison, associates the odor with "bitter berries . . . he must not eat" (106).

[42]

When their camp is overrun by the invaders, Nil and the old woman are killed, and "the new one" is taken away. At the end of Chapter 5, Lok is looking down at the water where his dead mother lies. The emotional effect is remarkable because of the absence of anything resembling mourning or lamentation. Lok's attitude toward the old woman was one of love mingled with awe, and it is fitting that his final remembrance of her should have a poignance tempered by restraint: "She was ignoring the injuries to her body, her mouth was open, the tongue showing and the specks of dirt were circling slowly in and out as though it had been nothing but a hole in a stone. Her eyes swept across the bushes, across his face, looked through him without seeing him, rolled away and were gone" (109).

With the reduction of the family to Lok and Fa, *The Inheritors* reaches midpoint; then the novel imperceptibly begins to shift its point of view. Lok and Fa, as well as the reader, are entering the world of Homo sapiens, and the more they become absorbed in the actions of the new people, the farther the novel drifts away from them until it finally becomes the property of the inheritors. The last half of the book is a moral reversal of the first, for the actions of Homo sapiens are in sharp contradistinction to those of the Neanderthals. Their religion is totemic and characterized by cannibalism and mutilation; they revere a witch doctor with an antlered mask. Their sex is explicit and adulterous, and their ritual climaxes in an orgy that Lok and Fa view with bemused fascination. In a scene marked by nervous, sardonic humor, the couple tries to imitate the new people. They drink their mead, and Lok for the first time discovers the simile and becomes enamored of it.

But such knowledge makes it impossible for the couple (and the novel) to return to the "delicious Paradise." The shift in emphasis to Homo sapiens has brought an accompanying shift in point of view. With the end of Chapter 11, the picture language of the Neanderthals is no longer operative; except for Lok, all have perished. Liku has been cannibalized, and Fa has drowned.

No longer is there talk of twigs for poison arrows, hollow logs for canoes, or dead snakes for whips; instead, there is the language of a people that has mastered the simile and triumphed over the crudities of metaphor (which is, ironically, the basis of poetry).

Lok has lost his identity as a person; to the postlapsarian observer he is, at the end of the chapter, a "red creature" described in animal terms. The personal pronoun is now the emasculated "it," and Lok's actions are those of a creature unworthy of gender or even remotely humane description. The creature trots, scrambles, sniffs, and staggers: "It was a strange creature, smallish, and bowed" (218–19). When Lok approaches the image which the new people had left, his is the quizzical wonder of a dog eying a toy replica of itself. Since Lok cannot fully understand his fate, he simply weeps, and his tears fall upon a withered leaf. Lok's death is almost canine in nature. He begins "to scramble in the earth" and with "the right forepaw" digs up a female-shaped root, the emblem of the goddess Oa, to whom he now returns. He approaches the waterfall where he assumes the position of a foetus and awaits absorption into Oa's womb. His return to the mother goddess is signaled by a collapse of the ice formations now melted by the sun. A new era dawns, but not without thundering chords that reverberate through the mountains and out toward the sea where the new people are.

The final chapter must be read with the close attention demanded by the first; both are really book ends enclosing the bulk of the action, and each complements the other. The novel begins with a family and ends with one. Instead of a group that shared a common identity, the new family comprises a ruthless despot, Marlan; a potential murderer, Tuami; a deranged child, Tanakil; and an adulterous mother, Vivani. Yet they have inherited the earth from Lok and will proceed to sow it accordingly. Although a sunburst christens their journey, it has occurred at the expense of a genocide.

Of the humans, only Tuami is haunted by the prospects of the journey he and his people are taking:

He [Tuami] rested his eyes on the back of his left hand and tried to think. He had hoped for the light as for a return to sanity and the manhood that seemed to have left them; but here was dawn—past dawn—and they were what they had been in the gap, haunted, bedevilled, full of strange irrational grief like himself, or emptied, collapsed, and helplessly asleep. . . . The world with the boat moving so slowly at the centre was dark amid the light, was untidy, hopeless, dirty (224–25).

The boat is a symbol of the progress of Homo sapiens, of a continual journey which can only be painted in chiaroscuro. At the very end of the book Tuami gazes at the line of darkness along the horizon, but it does not seem to have an ending. Nor, as Golding believes, does the line of darkness that perpetually oscillates in man's heart.

The Inheritors is a difficult but a rewarding work; it possesses the allusiveness of a modern poem, rich in imagery that envelops the naked structure like lush foliage. Of all the Golding novels, it is the most successful at defying a line of demarcation between poetry and artistic prose, for the work has a definite image pattern. Light alternates with darkness to create a world roofed in by shadow, occasionally shot with sun. But the imagery is not separated from character; the Neanderthal mind is similar to the shadowy paradise in which "the people" live—misty, adumbrated by undefined memories, and sometimes illuminated by pictures.

Lok and his tribe are very like the uneducated of Plato's *Republic*—shackled in a cave, they view reality only in terms of flickering reflections on the wall. Consequently, much of the action takes place at night, often by a smoking fire. The first chapter ends with a sunset, and "shadows . . . racing through the gap towards the terrace" (29). The sun sets frequently in *The Inheritors,* and with it comes the departure of light. Lok's premonition of "something else" on the island occurs in an eerie moonlight. Mal is illumined by the setting sun "so that shadows stretched from him to the other end of the fire" (63–64). He is also buried at night. As Lok and Fa go in search of Liku, "their bodies wove a parallel skein of shadows" (118). They possess "night sight" and can therefore make their way through the underbrush to the camp of the new people. Lok dies in twilight that turns his red body gray and blue. Significantly, the novel ends with Tuami looking at the unending line of darkness.

Readers who question a novelist's attraction for Neanderthal man would do well to read "Digging for Pictures," which provides an even better background for *The Inheritors* than Wells's *Outline.*[5] As a youngster Golding did some excavating and came upon the bones of a family from "the days of innocence" and something that might have been the head of a doll; one thinks immediately of "the little Oa." It was one of those experiences that leaves an indelible impression on a young artist and can only result in the production of a novel or a poem, and *The Inheritors* is both. Unfortunately, the results of his digging were covered over by a bulldozer making a runway, causing what the author calls "a prehistoric murder." Yet, Golding reflects, contact with the bones of that family has "taken something of me with them."

One can readily understand how a child's initial confrontation with the prehistoric past can supply the first strands of a web that will be eventually woven into a novel. More important, however, the essay crystallizes much of what Golding feels about the loss of innocence. There is a delicious temptation to see the young Golding as a prototype of Ralph, who watches his newly found world of bones and artifacts entombed forever by a bulldozer. One would also like to think of Lok as the author's *persona.* "For most of us, though," Golding observes, "history is not diagrams—however accurate—but pictures. . . ." Lok and his family can only think in pictures ("I have a picture") which contain the history of their race and become externalized in artifacts.

Golding considers *The Inheritors* his finest novel, and it is not difficult to see why. Although he is still preoccupied with the two worlds, two wisdoms polarity, his statement of it is far less simplistic than in *Lord of the Flies* because he makes no philosophical concessions: he refuses to isolate evil in any one character, not even Tuami, who is as pitiful a figure as Lok. Lok has at least returned to the womb of his mother goddess, but Tuami must embark on a perilous journey in a *bateau ivre* against a horizon that can promise no light.

Like Herodotus, who had words of praise for both Greek and barbarian, Golding is also unbiased. In their journey into darkness "the new people" require almost as much compassion as the Neanderthals; they are, after all, ourselves, and the final chapter is a mirror for the reader. Tuami realizes that progress always occurs at another's expense, but " 'What else could we have done?' " (227). He would like to murder Marlan, his rival for Vivani's affections, and begins to sharpen a piece of ivory into a point. But he soon stops: "Who would sharpen a point against the darkness of the world?" (231).

Vivani, who may have played the whore earlier with Tuami, can still be maternal to the Neanderthal child on board, even though it is now a "red devil." This specter of the past may frighten her, but she does not deny it a mother's affection: "He sniffed, turned, ran at Vivani's leg and scrambled up to her breast. She was shuddering and laughing as if this pleasure and love were also a fear and a torment. The devil's hands and feet had laid hold of her. Hesitating, half-ashamed, with that same frightened laughter, she bent her head, cradled him with her arms and shut her eyes" (230–31).

The Neanderthals are clearly not the heroes, nor are the new people the villains of the novel, for they belong to the same genus —man. Therefore, our Mousterian ancestors are not guilty of introducing polygamy, murder, idolatry, and mutilation, for man has had a capacity for these evils from the moment of his existence. What Golding is saying is that the "true men," as Wells called them in the *Outline,* if they are supposed to tower over the rest of creation, should be capable of using their intellect to quell these dark, demonic urges; but in fact they are less able to cope with them than their Neanderthal brothers. Each rung on the evolutionary ladder brings additional knowledge, but there is always a price for it.

It is significant that the humans take a Neanderthal child with them on their ominous voyage. They regard it as a "red devil" and indeed this is how Homo sapiens considers his brutish ancestors: *they* are the bedeviled ones, the cannibals, the idolators—not he. But the real devil, the real ogre, lies in the heart of man *qua* man. It is impossible to separate the shadow from the one who casts it.

CHAPTER 4

After the First Death

"Christopher Hadley Martin had no belief in anything but the importance of his own life; no love, no God. Because he was created in the image of God he had a freedom of choice which he used to centre the world on himself. He did not believe in purgatory and therefore when he died it was not presented to him in overtly theological terms. The greed for life which had been the mainspring of his nature, forced him to refuse the selfless act of dying. He continued to exist in a world composed of his own murderous nature. His drowned body lies rolling in the Atlantic but the ravenous ego invents a rock for him to endure on. It is the memory of an aching tooth. Ostensibly and rationally he is a survivor from a torpedoed destroyer: but deep down he knows the truth. He is not fighting for bodily survival but for his continuing identity in the face of what will smash it and sweep it away—the black lightning, the compassion of God. For Christopher, the Christ-bearer, has become Pincher Martin who is little but greed. Just to be Pincher is purgatory; to be Pincher for eternity is hell."

—WILLIAM GOLDING, on *Pincher Martin*

IN *Pincher Martin* (1956) Golding attempts to blend an adventure tale which requires a straightforward narration with a series of flashbacks, or "memory scenes," that are fragmentary and elusive. The form he has chosen is deceptively simple; reduced to its barest essentials it is the story of Christopher Hadley Martin, the sole survivor of a British warship, the *Wildebeeste*, that is torpedoed in the Atlantic during World War II. In the beginning, Martin is apparently drowning; and in the end a British officer, again "hunting" (this time for destroyed ships), recovers his dead body. Between the description of the drowning and the final chapter, it appears that Martin had been miraculously saved by his lifebelt; he is then cast up on a rock island where he recalls experiences of his past life and where he magnificently combats hunger, sickness, and the elements in a determined effort to survive.

But the recovery of the body seems to nullify the whole point of the novel which is largely concerned with Martin's struggle for existence. This seeming inconsistency is only clarified if one remembers that *Martin had died within minutes of the torpedoing* and that the major part of the book describes an afterlife that he undergoes. The beginning is only understood in terms of the end, and the movement of the novel is comparable to the calculated tracing of a circle that takes on intelligibility only when the curve is finally closed. To understand the book, the reader must retrace the curve of the circle from its starting point and view the end in terms of the beginning.

There is no doubt that on the very first page Golding is describing a drowning: "When the air had gone with the shriek, water came in to fill its place—burning water, hard in the throat and mouth as stones that hurt" (7).[1] Martin then kicks off his seaboots ("Both boots had left him." [10]) and inflates his lifebelt ("He blew deeply and regularly into the tube until the lifebelt rose . . ." [11]). But in the last chapter, Mr. Campbell, the Scottish crofter who found Martin's body, remarks: "'Those are wicked things, those lifebelts. They give a man hope when there is no longer any call for it. They are cruel'" (207). And the final line of the novel makes it quite clear that the survival was hallucinatory: "'You saw the body. He didn't even have time to kick off his seaboots'" (208).[2] Therefore, the entire action of the novel, except for the opening and final chapter, has taken place in that no man's land between death and judgment.

The structure of the book might then be considered as follows:

A. The Drowning (7–8). It is evident that, with the half-formed word "Mother" ('"Moth—'"), Martin is dead.

B. The Purgatory (9–201). Memory scenes of his past life alternate with his struggle for survival in a highly metaphorical present, culminating in his annihilation by black lightning.

C. The Aftermath of the Drowning (Chapter 14: 202–8). Mr. Davidson, a captain in the British navy, arrives on an island in the Outer Hebrides to claim Martin's body which had been washed up on shore.

Although the narrative structure of *Pincher Martin* is easily plotted, it would be foolish to make the outline a substitute for the work itself. Golding is not writing a melodrama; if he were, the episodes would link themselves together into a totality that would provide its own explanation. The narrative framework is really like a scaffold—necessary but removable once the building is completed. The reader must first adhere rigidly to the details of the plot; he must accept the presence on a rock island in mid-Atlantic of Martin, who is fighting to survive the onslaughts of nature. In fact, Golding facilitates such acceptance by his realistic descriptions such as the touching of moist objects and the cracking of mussel shells; there is such an emphasis on the sensory that one experiences the physical and tactile reactions along with Martin. But, at the end of the novel, the reader should be able to stand outside the plot and view it dispassionately. Again, Golding does not make this impossible: the rock island is not transformed into anything other than it was, but it can now be seen as a symbol, as a projection of Martin's petrified nature. What was literal during the reading becomes symbolic in the analysis.

It is true that the ending is "gimmicked" and that it is possible to feel cheated by it.[3] If the reader feels tricked (and what is operative is not a practical joke, but rather a meaningful narrative device designed to jolt one's sense of moral awareness), he should recall the theatricality of the main character which will determine much of what he does. Prior to entering the navy, Martin was an actor. The roles that he played in civilian life are of considerable importance in establishing his character. In a morality play he is given the part of Greed, and everyone including Pete, the producer, and Helen, his wife, who was also Martin's mistress, agree that it is the perfect role for someone like himself "'born with his mouth and his flies open and both hands out to grab'" (120). His repertoire mirrors his personality: Danny, the psychopath of Emlyn Williams' *Night Must Fall;* the witty sybarite Algernon in Wilde's *The Importance of Being Earnest;* Freddy, presumably of Shaw's *Pygmalion;* Demetrius in Shakespeare's *A Midsummer Night's Dream;* and, although his role in Congreve's *The Way of the World* is never specified (it may have been Mirabell), it is easy to imagine Martin's substituting a leer for the brittle wit of the Restoration comedy.

Furthermore, Golding often writes stage directions for his hero. For example, in Chapter 12 there is a portentous episode between Martin and his friend, Nathaniel. Just before the ship is torpedoed, Martin sees Nat leaning on the rail. He is repelled by everything that Nathaniel represents—his simplistic piety which makes him a kinsman of Simon, but in particular his affection for Mary Lovell, whom Martin desires only in terms of animal lust. He cannot differentiate between Nat and Mary, for both have qualities that clash dissonantly with Martin's hedonism. Nathaniel suggests his guileless biblical counterpart (John 1:47), and the very name, Mary Lovell, recalls a benign Madonna. Thinking that by destroying one he will obliterate the other from his mind, Martin plans his diabolical scheme.

At this point Golding enters the action as omniscient narrator (or better, director), plotting the action with a pace that grows progressively more accelerated, and giving his actor the proper staging to carry him through the scene. First Martin dismisses all witnesses. The directions read: "Feet descending the ladder. . . . Ham it a bit. Casual saunter to the port side. Pause" (185–86). Martin is then to cross to the voice pipe and cry, "'Hard a-starboard for Christ's sake!'" presuming that Nat will be swept off the rail. Again he is given the necessary staging: "Scramble to the binnacle, fling yourself at the voice pipe, voice urgent . . ." (186). Ironically, the order coincided with the torpedoing, but Martin is not consumed with recriminations: "'And it was the right bloody order!'" (186).

When he uses the lifebelt to give himself an enema, it is done with a mixture of realism and fantasy that characterizes so much of the novel. The basic act of defecation is done to a scenario that calls for music from Tchaikovsky, Wagner, and Holst. One is to imagine a surrealistic film, something like Disney's *Fantasia,* with swirling colors and extravagantly romantic music, punctuated by a blast from Martin's bowels. The setting is supplied for him; he has merely to stand within it and perform.

As soon as he is washed up on the rock island, he begins to play a role he had never performed onstage—the Odyssean hero, resourceful, wily, and indestructible. He finds his own food—mussels and anemones—suffers ptomaine poisoning from them, and proceeds to construct his own world with all of Ralph's tidy rationalism in *Lord of the Flies:* " 'I call this place the Look-out. That is the Dwarf. The rock out there under the sun where I came swimming is Safety Rock. The place where I get mussels and stuff is Food Cliff. Where I eat them is—The Red Lion. On the south side where the strap-weed is, I call Prospect Cliff' " (84). To put a label on one's environment is to control it, and Martin uses this eternal logic presumably to dispel fear of the unknown. But a self-conscious rationalism does not satisfy him, and it soon becomes apparent that he is really trying to blot out the growing realization that the island is not what it should be.

Golding allows his hero to play other roles on the rock island which he could never perform in life. In Chapter 13 he has written a bravura mad scene that would have been completely beyond the capabilities of Christopher Martin, juvenile lead. But there is one *caveat:* the reader must remember that Martin the shipwrecked figure differs at times from Martin the hedonist actor; and he must always keep in mind what the *real* Martin was. Golding has carefully supplied the biographical data, but he has done so in a series of highly fragmented memory scenes presented without any chronological order.

The device of reminiscence can be a very clear and articulate one, as it is in Tennessee Williams' *The Glass Menagerie* where the narrator, Tom Wingfield, recalls scenes of his family life in St.

Louis with remarkable clarity. But Golding is not asking the reader to enter the mind of someone who is sufficiently detached from his past to view it with objectivity; he requires that one plunge himself into the mental vortex of a lifeless man. The "memory scenes" in *Pincher Martin* are at first difficult to comprehend and frequently seem even unintelligible. Names are introduced literally out of nowhere—Pete, Helen, Nathaniel. But Golding is telling a conventional tale in an unconventional way, and therefore cannot use the traditional means to present his *dramatis personae*. The seeming lack of clarity in these episodes is not faulty technique on Golding's part; they are the half-in-light, half-in-shadow recollections of a man who is midway between death and judgment.

From these "memory scenes" a clear picture of Christopher Martin emerges. His entire life has been devoted to consuming people; indeed, Martin is preoccupied with the idea of eating: "Think about eating women, eating men, crunching up Alfred . . ." (90). His theater friends regard him in the same way. One of them, Pete, the producer, recounts a tale about the preparation of a Chinese delicacy. A fish is buried in a tin box; soon maggots consume the fish, then one another, until finally one maggot alone emerges. Pincher is the maggot triumphant who can cry with the exultation of a victorious child, "I'm a bigger maggot than you are" (153).

Even his name is suggestive of his character, but in this instance Golding demands multiple levels of interpretation. On the one hand, his name is Christopher Martin; and, like his namesake, the third-century saint, he is also making a precarious journey across the water as a spiritual preparation. On the other, he is a Martin in the Royal Navy where all Martin's are nicknamed "Pincher," just as every Mullins in the American army is "Moon Mullins." On still another level, he is *Pincher* Martin—Greed, the successful maggot—constantly grasping whatever comes within his reach.

Within the course of the novel he has blatantly seduced two women, raped another, and engaged in a "crude and unsatisfactory experiment" in homosexuality. In one memory scene he reenacts a bedroom farce with Sibyl and Alfred. He then proceeds to take his producer's wife, Helen, as his mistress. Along with his need to satiate his ego with people is the desire to destroy whatever is his opposite—particularly Nathaniel whom he seeks to murder, and Mary, whom he rapes.

Nathaniel is only sketchily drawn (as indeed are all the characters of the "memory scenes"), but Golding has given him the most important words in the novel. Nathaniel is a mystic like Simon in *Lord of the Flies;* there are similarities since each has somehow transcended the mundane in an environment not especially conducive to spirituality. But Nat is much more articulate about his religious commitment. He may be a grown-up Simon, but the maturing process has made all the difference between a child who must confront evil in a state of mute understanding and a man who has retained his childhood innocence but can speak convincingly on the four ultimates: death, judgment, heaven, and hell.

Nat has a twofold function in the novel; he is clearly the author's mouthpiece conveying a philosophy of death in a form that is more poetic than that of the ordinary catechism. One must achieve the ability to die *into* heaven (71), almost as if heaven were simply a state after life, and one passes into it the same way one goes from boyhood to adulthood—a smooth, unbroken crossing. " 'Take us as we are now and heaven would be sheer negation. Without form and void. You see? A sort of black lightning, destroying everything that we call life—' " (183).

But more important, Nat is Martin's warner. On two occasions, Nat suggests, in speaking of eternity, what will happen to Martin if he does not prepare himself for "dying into heaven." In the first instance, he feebly prophesies Martin's death; but, because he is a visionary motivated by love and suffering, he cannot finish the sentence: " 'because in only a few years—' " (71). The enraged Martin does complete the sentence, but only out of defiance and rage that such words should be uttered against one who is the life force itself. When Nat again speaks of life as a preparation for eternity, he alludes to a "black lightning" that will destroy those who pattern an afterlife on their own natures. Christopher Martin is such a person and, prophetically enough, will be annihilated by this black lightning.

But what has been described is the Martin of the "memory scenes," the Martin of the past who lied and seduced his way through life. We must now consider the Martin who grapples with epic indignities on the rock island.

I *The Bound Promethean*

The Martin on Rockall (the name he has given to his island home) belongs to the realm of myth. Definitions of myth are almost as numerous as its definers, but it is generally agreed that, as a literary term, it refers to a subject that is so sublimated that it is recognizable to everyone. Thus Martin on Rockall strikes a responsive chord to anyone familiar with "survival literature," from the *Odyssey* to the most recent science fiction. One can see elements common to all survival novels present in *Pincher Martin:* man versus the elements, man in search of food and shelter, and man attempting to inject some sort of order into the chaos of his island environment. But here the similarities cease, for Golding goes far beyond the techniques of the survival novel into the realm of what might be called "anti-myth."

Anti-myth is essentially a parody of myth in which the writer identifies his character with certain heroes of the past, allowing him to possess some of their qualities, but in a negative way. For example, just before he is destroyed by the apocalyptic black lightning, Martin cries, " 'I am Atlas. I am Prometheus' "; and again, " 'Ajax! Prometheus!' " It would be easy to pass over these names as mere maniacal ravings, but Golding, who uses an economy of words to achieve his effect, does not insert proper names as Classical ornaments. In ancient mythology, Atlas was punished for his role in the rebellion of the Titans by being forced to hold up the heavens with his head and hands. Like his Greek counterpart, Martin is also limited to the confines of the rock world, hemmed in by earth and sky. Ajax, the Greek warrior in the *Iliad,* yearned for Achilles' armor only to lose it to Odysseus; then Ajax went mad and in his frenzy killed a flock of sheep that he imagined were the Greek leaders. In the final part of the novel, Martin also goes mad, but his madness is a self-induced solace to ward off the growing fear that the whole experience may be delusive. Ajax invaded a flock of sheep, but Martin can only break the backs of mussels with an adolescent sadism.

But Golding uses names whose meanings are not exhausted by one interpretation. It is possible that he wishes to convey a further dimension of Martin's character by linking him with another Ajax. There was "the lesser Ajax," who forced the virgin priestess Cassandra away from her temple and raped her. Shipwrecked on his homeward journey from Troy, he managed to swim ashore where he boasted that he saved himself despite the gods. His arrogance infuriated Poseidon, the sea divinity, who killed him by hurling into the sea the rock on which he stood. The allusion is quite apt; for, like the lesser Ajax, Martin was a shipwrecked sailor and a rapist. In the final pages of the novel he also defies God, who in turn annihilates him. Only after the novel is finished can one see how ironic the invoking of Ajax's name was.

Prometheus, the Titan who stole fire to aid man, was imprisoned by Zeus on a cliff. When he refused to tell Zeus the name of the mortal who would some day overthrow him, he was swallowed up by an earthquake amid thunder and lightning. Martin also defies God, but cannot address him with Promethean eloquence. Prometheus cries:

> In face of this I defy the flame
> Of the flickering tongue of the lightning flash.
> Let it strike two-forked, let the thunder crash,
> Let the wild typhoon and the hurricane
> Disrupt the space of the sky. Let shock
> Of air imprisoned blast rock from rock,
> And tear the infernal roots apart
> Till the whole earth quake to its very heart,
>
> . . . .
>
> Whatever the peril, the doom, the pain,
> Self-existent I still remain.
> Zeus's hand can never destroy me.[4]

Martin can only scream, " 'I spit on your compassion!' " In a magnificent parody on the end of Aeschylus' *Prometheus Bound,* black lightning sunders earth from sky accompanied by Martin's raging rejection, " 'I shit on your heaven!' "

Before his annihilation, Golding gives Martin the chance to play *King Lear,* but it is to be the role of the bastard Edgar, not the title part: "There was still a part that could be played—there was the Bedlamite, Poor Tom . . ." (177–78). In fact, Golding has invented some verses that sound oddly reminiscent of the Shakespearean tragedy: *"Rage, roar, and spout!/ Let us have wind, rain, hail, gouts of blood / Storms and tornadoes. . . ."*

A composite of the physical endurance of Atlas, the brutishness of Ajax, the defiance of Prometheus and the feigned madness of Edgar, Martin lacks their corresponding heroic qualities. Layers of mythic dimension have been put one on another to make up Christopher Martin on Rockall. He is a manufactured hero, not a born one. But, since he was not created for heroism, his only claim to stature is to enact it.

Martin was an actor, and his final destruction is completely theatrical. At the end, after his rejection of God's mercy, the painted canvas disintegrates like the magic garden in Wagner's *Parsifal,* and Martin is hurled into a waiting eternity. That Golding envisioned a theatrical ending with the collapse of flats and backdrops can be seen from his description: "The sea stopped moving, froze, became paper, painted paper that was torn by a black line. The rock was painted on the same paper. The whole of the painted sea was tilted but nothing ran downhill into the black crack which had opened in it" (200).

There are probably some readers who feel that the novel should end with Martin's annihilation and not with the recovery of his body. But since *Pincher Martin* has been shown to be a theater piece, the ending is apropos. Artists do not trick their public, and there is no doubt that Golding belongs to this category. One may have been mildly deceived, but the deception was wrought by a skilled hand. The reader has witnessed the enactment of a play within a play, a monodrama with the character repeating scenes from his past life and rehearsing new roles to fit the occasion. In the end, the backdrop is swept away, and the reader is hurled out of the realm of the illusory into the world of real death.

The structure of *Pincher Martin* is very much akin to a modern poem; it is, in academic parlance, "difficult," and the ending is only understandable when the whole novel is viewed in retrospect. Once the ending is understood, the seeming inconsistencies really emerge as part of a carefully constructed fabric whose threads at times seem to cross fortuitously but are actually under the control of a skilled hand.

For reasons more logical than literary, the final chapter is not at odds with the rest of the book. Golding has incorporated several clues about the real nature of Martin's "death" into the narrative; these, too, must be considered in retrospect. First, there has clearly been a drowning as even a cursory reading of the first page will show. The author has vividly described the separation of soul and body, but his eschatology is not quite so simple. Christopher Martin was so vital a personality, endowed with such a lust for life, that his death could not result from something so mundane as drowning. His complete destruction can only be wrought at the hands of God.

Drowning has merely brought about a temporary cleavage of matter and spirit, but what Christopher Martin is essentially—a snarl—remains: "Could he have controlled the nerves of his face, or could a face have been fashioned to fit the attitude of his consciousness where it lay suspended between life and death that face would have worn a snarl" (8). Drowning cannot obliterate an essence, and what endures is just that—his essence in the form of a snarl, a muscularly contorted view of the world. The snarl then remains—Golding is quite clear on this point—and for the sake of the fictional convention which cannot allow characters to function as disembodied spirits, the snarl becomes humanized, attired in recognizable form. Thus, Golding has not really tricked the reader; he has described a drowning, but he has also shown that the indomitable essence of a person cannot be snuffed out by water alone.

It would not be sufficient for the reader alone to know of the unusual fate of Christopher Martin; the protagonist must also be aware of it, if the horror of his living purgatory is to have any meaning. Here again Golding does not fail. Toward the end of the novel, Martin sees a red lobster with which he now becomes identified: " 'Whoever saw a lobster like that swimming in the sea? A red lobster?' " (167). A sudden horror grips him because lobsters are red only when boiled. Random thoughts race through his mind: Is he dead? Is there someone else on the rock? Is he mad? Soon he is struck by another realization: guano, the manure of sea birds, is insoluble. If this is the case, then it would be impossible for such "slimy wetness" to exist.

Another series of clues artfully prepares the way for the final symbolic identification of Martin with a lobster. The lobster claws, to which he is finally reduced, have been mentioned earlier (59) when he peered into a trench that contained crab shells, dead weed, and "the claws of a lobster." Earlier in the book, Martin saw a lobster, and the sight repelled him. It is ironic that he should be repulsed by his closest counterpart in the animal world, a creature whose claws are always extended with pincing movements. He is finally reduced to a pair of lobster claws, a fitting metamorphosis for one who seized everything he wanted in life.

Golding's technique has thus far been masterful. Without hoodwinking the reader, he has taken him into an illusory experience, allowing him to share the mythical realism by a wealth of vivid, sensory detail. Nor has he abandoned him in the most harrowing moment of the tale: the reader is right there in Martin's mind. Both learn at the same time that the survival was illusory. The rest of the novel, except for the final chapter, follows with an inexorable consistency: Martin, now aware that he is neither among the dead nor the living, must react to this new-found knowledge.

After he has exercised his formidable rationalism by naming the various districts on Rockall, he is about to name three rocks "the Teeth." He immediately recoils at the thought: " 'No! Not the Teeth!' " (91). Christopher Martin, the human mouth that reveled in masticating people, is now afraid to impart a name to the rocks, for naming them would bring a knowledge of what they represent. He then tries to sleep, but cannot. The horror that he is now enclosed within teeth and the realization that Rockall is shaped along the contours of a mouth slowly impinge upon his mind. He must answer his own question: he cannot sleep because "Sleep is where we touch what is best left unexamined." But Martin must keep his senses continually alert so that the grim reality never reaches him. He cannot admit to himself that he is Rockall, a petrified mass in a boundless sea, for such an admission would destroy all the pretense of his glorious survival. To avoid such horrifying implications, he chooses to play a mad scene and to parody dialogue from *King Lear*.

Martin's destruction is not so much an aspect of Golding's technique as an outgrowth of what has preceded. Golding's art is really invisible; the character and his situation determine the outcome. The author has only to guide the narrative along. Given the nature of Christopher Martin, the final pages of Chapter 13 are inevitable. Only God can impart a sentence; an epiphany is warranted and occurs with the utmost naturalness.

In the final episode Martin confronts God appropriately dressed as a seaman. Now approaching his climax, Golding dispels any doubt that this is a mere survival story. God's question and Martin's reply make this clear:

> "Have you had enough, Christopher?"
> . . . .
> "Enough of what?"
> "Surviving. Hanging on" (194–95).

Now the real death occurs; thus, when the novel was published in the United States the following year, it bore the title, *The Two Deaths of Christopher Martin,* which had a neat literalness about it, but not the author's sanction. Not even Martin's animal extremities, the lobster claws, are spared; he must be reduced to complete nothingness by black lightning, not by the Miltonic red (*Paradise Lost* 1, 175) that is reserved for fallen angels. For Martin, life alone was all that mattered; he lived on because, as Nat observed, he never learned how to die. The voracious ego could survive something as commonplace as drowning; it cannot, however, survive annihilation.

CHAPTER 5

Our Meddling Intellect

"I am by nature an optimist; but a defective logic—or a logic which I sometimes hope desperately is defective—makes a pessimist of me."
—WILLIAM GOLDING, "On the Crest of the Wave"

GOLDING'S prose at its best is comparable to a mosaic, each part delicately set off against the other, and the whole produces a dazzling configuration. The lapidary style can only be achieved by a verbal asceticism, a refusal to say more than is absolutely necessary, and by an insistence upon language that has been pruned of all imperfections. This economy of words has found its fullest expression in the "diamond-hard, diamond-exact" kind of novel of which Golding is so fond; it has also led him into the novella, the short story, the play and radio drama, but thus far not with overwhelming success. He has written one full-length work for the stage, *The Brass Butterfly* (1958), which is really a dramatization of his novella *Envoy Extraordinary* (1956). It is the sort of play that Little Theatre and college groups would attempt largely on the strength of the author's name; but, unless it finds an audience that accepts a peculiar blend of high comedy, melodrama, and cynicism, *The Brass Butterfly* remains an anthologist's heirloom, like Joyce's *Exiles*.

Golding starts with a premise that was later to intrigue Swiss playwright Friedrich Duerrenmatt, in *Romulus the Great:* a Roman emperor compounded of mythic and semi-historical strains (Golding's emperor is fictitious but suggests something of cross between Trajan and Marcus Aurelius; Duerrenmatt's is Romulus Augustulus, the last of the Caesars) whose effete and scatterbrained exterior conceals a fear of progress and a distrust of human beings. The emperor in *The Brass Butterfly* has retired to Capri where his holiday is interrupted by Phanocles, a Greek rationalist with the detached clarity of vision that his name implies. The Greek is an inventor and invites the emperor to sample his pressure cooker, steamship, and explosive missile. Caesar, the epicure, is delighted with the pressure cooker but is wary of the others.

The action is further complicated by the rivalry between Postumus, the heir designate, and Mamillius, the emperor's poetic but illegitimate grandson. When the steam engine literally devours Postumus' ships, the infuriated general uses the Greek's missile to storm the villa. But Euphrosyne, Phanocles' sister, removes the arming vane, the brass butterfly of the title, thereby causing the projectile to explode and kill Postumus. Mamillius, who had become attracted to Euphrosyne, asks for her in marriage and converts to Christianity. The emperor is left shaken by the day's events and what they presage. But for Phanocles, new scientific horizons are already expanding. He envisions a compass, a printing press, and public libraries; and he is about to tamper with the earth's productivity when the wily emperor dubs him Envoy Extraordinary and consigns him to a slow boat to China.

The Brass Butterfly is the sort of playfully serious comedy that a Classicist by training and a moralist by avocation would create. The techniques of Classical drama—the unified action, the Terentian double plot, the messenger's report of the off-stage violence of the steam engine—come to Golding with an effortlessness that stems from familiarity. They are natural to him and to the play.

Again Golding works from a polarity: the scientist is as singleminded about improving mankind with inventions as the emperor is about saving it with an ineffectual humanism. But, in this case, the polarity does not arise from a Tower of Babel where voices cry out in opposition without the gift of tongues. Phanocles cannot understand his master's wary conservatism; but the emperor, while he cannot accept the consequences of science, knows all too well that it is man who can transform a steam engine designed for navigation into a dynamo of death:

PHANOCLES: Caesar, I conquered the universe, and yet the ants have defeated me. What is wrong with man?
EMPEROR: Men. A steam ship, or anything powerful, in the hands of man, Phanocles, is like a sharp knife in the hands of a child. There is nothing wrong with the knife. There is nothing wrong with the steam ship. There is nothing wrong with man's intelligence. The trouble is his nature[1] (Act III).

At first the emperor's position baffles and irritates. He speaks like a hardened sophist, quibbling about singular and plural because he views the species as a corruption of the genus. He cannot see that a genus requires a species for its realization, and a species in turn demands divergences in its members. One cannot avoid the consequences of incarnation, however much it may sully the ideal nature.

Although the emperor exasperates the reader with his uncomfortable Platonism, he is essentially a human figure—a saddened humanist, a disbeliever in men, and a clinger to old gods. One is tempted to view the Caesar as Golding's finest self-portrait. Dramatically, the reader accepts the emperor's dilemma precisely because he accepts it himself. If the emperor had merely said that men subvert man, one would regard him only as a wearisome misanthrope. But he goes on to state the rather common philosophical view that scientific invention is amoral and, like everything else, can be used for good or ill. There is nothing controversial or profound about the emperor's position; in fact, it is unstartlingly orthodox.

Golding is not a bumbling reformer who leaves the audience in a state of bewilderment, clamoring for a tidy resolution. There is no solution to the problem of human nature, especially in a three-act "comedy of ideas." If a playwright has opened a wound, the best he can do is close it painlessly in the final scene. Here Golding has conjured up all the magic of stagecraft to create a twilight that is now more gentle than ominous. A eunuch sings, and harp music filters in from the veranda. The comedy which began with the bubbling Mamillius diligently working out the metrics of a love poem terminates with the old emperor meditating on what scientific discovery will mean for man. The events of the day have chastened him; he no longer speaks in frivolities, but with a bittersweet wisdom.

But the humanist is always cleverer than the literal-minded scientist; and, while the emperor can laugh at himself and his idealism, he will not be defeated. And thus the gilding of the pill begins. Phanocles will take the slow boat to China and scientific advancement will be deferred. The audience can breathe more freely now. The play is a comedy and one leaves with the feeling that, whenever destruction is imminent, there will always be a *deus ex machina,* whose forms, as Euripides liked to point out, are many and could conceivably include an extended sea voyage.

The play, it should be remembered, has a dream-like atmosphere. Euphrosyne walks about in a trance-like state and says she was directed to remove the brass butterfly as if in a dream. In the final scene, the emperor asks Phanocles if he had dreamed the day's events. The play has the effect of a misshapen fantasy where individuals are caught up in the waves of fitful melodrama, tossed about and wrenched out of shape, and returned to wholeness with the jolting sobriety of waking. The emperor too is the stuff that dreams are made on. He may have played the fool, and in a sense he still does right up to the final curtain. But fools, as Erasmus has shown, can still be wise; and, when the emperor creates Phanocles Envoy Extraordinary, he is no longer the proverbial bell without a clapper. The sound is now quite resonant. The motley does not completely cover his practical toga.

CHAPTER 6

The Awful Rainbow

"Any man who claims to have found a bridge between the world of the physical sciences and the world of the spirit is sure of a hearing. Is this not because most of us have an unexpressed faith that the bridge exists, even if we have not the wit to discover it?"

—WILLIAM GOLDING, "All or Nothing"

I *Mixing Memory with Desire*

IF one can imagine a Christopher Martin with the capacity for salvation (Martin was damned from the outset), such a person would be Sammy Mountjoy, the narrator of *Free Fall* (1959). Like his solipsistic brother, he relives incidents from his life, but with this difference: Martin must take part in a foreordained ritual that demands a re-enactment of the past just prior to the separation of soul from body; Sammy voluntarily engages in memory therapy and, by conjuring up fragments of his past, tries to give some form to his directionless present. In such a purgation, detail is of the utmost importance; no memory is left untouched; no incident is too irrelevant: smells, moods, colors assume an almost inordinate immediacy when a character is retracing the steps that led to his spiritual malaise. Sammy is seeking an answer to one burning question: "When did I lose my freedom?" (5).[1] After each remembered episode, he asks, "Here?"; and the reply, until the end of Chapter 12, is negative.

His earliest recollections are of his childhood in a Kentish slum, Rotten Row. Plagued by his illegitimacy ("'What was my dad, Ma?'"), he finds little consolation in the conflicting versions of his whorish but good-natured mother. Since he is the typical fatherless boy, it is natural that his first recollections are of the female: Maggie, whom he sees while playing with a matchbox in the gutter; Evie, who fashioned her own world of make-believe and reveled in thoughts of urination; and Minnie, who relieves herself in the classroom with a complete lack of inhibition. In themselves, these experiences are undistinguished and even commonplace, but they repeat themselves—as, indeed, many of his childhood relationships do—in later life.

As Sammy matures and begins to move out of the world of Rotten Row, his female-oriented associations evolve into boy friendships. His two main female influences, Ma and Evie, are exchanged for two male ones, Philip and Johnny. Sammy's actions become characteristically boyish—a nighttime excursion to an airport, trespassing on a general's estate, bullying younger boys. None of these events is particularly significant, and at the end of the first memory scene Sammy still has not found the point he has been seeking: "No. Not here" (52).

In the second memory scene, Philip dares him to urinate on a church altar, but Sammy is only able to spit. He is caught by the latently homosexual Father Watts-Watt, who adopts Sammy after his mother dies. As Sammy closes this phase of his boyhood, he asks, " 'Well. There?' " (70); but the answer is again negative.

The next recollection explores Sammy's first encounter with Beatrice. Now nineteen, an art student and a member of the Communist Party, Sammy has had his first experience with sex and wishes to continue it with Beatrice, whom he seduces and abandons after he realizes that she is frigid. Again the moment eludes him: " 'No. Not here' " (132).

World War II and imprisonment in a concentration camp fail to supply the answer to what is now a recurrent rhetorical question. Finally, he recalls the words of his headmaster on graduation day: " 'If you want something enough, you can always get it provided you are willing to make the appropriate sacrifice' " (235). Sammy wanted Beatrice and was willing to sacrifice everything: "Here?" The question is never answered because it would be foolish to belabor the obvious. But Beatrice, who found her initiation into sex comparable to an innoculation, ends her days in a mental hospital, babbling incoherently and urinating with infantile abandon.

II   *Assessment*

The critical reception accorded to *Free Fall* was at best lukewarm, although the novel was highly touted prior to publication.[2] One undistinguished novel will not denigrate Golding's stature, but its faults merit discussion since they represent decidedly real pitfalls for writers who choose this particular form. First, there is something shopworn about the technique, and one sees too clearly what is being done. Sammy is always surrounded by pairs of people; his childhood fixations, Ma and Evie, yield to boyhood friends, Johnny and Philip, who in turn merge into Alsopp and Wimbury, his adult comrades in the Party. His sex life was satisfied by Beatrice and Taffy. His secondary school influences were also dominated by two extremes: Nick Shales, the atheistic scientist, and Miss Pringle, the neurotic religion teacher.

One might argue that Sammy's lack of self-awareness necessitates the presence of twin guardian angels, but the characters hardly serve that function. All are presumably threads in the fabric of his life, but they align themselves in pairs not so much because of fictional circumstances but because the author has chosen this particular way. One does not argue with the hand that is in control of the loom; one can only point out the blatant sameness in the pattern.

In one instance Golding is successful in linking Sammy's past with his present. After the war Sammy learns that Beatrice is in a mental institution and visits her. Chapter 13 is successful because it connects three seemingly unrelated episodes: the youthful escapade to the general's house, Minnie's spontaneous urination in the classroom, and Beatrice's fear of madness. The general's house is now a mental institution, and Beatrice's fear of insanity has now become a reality. Moreover, her psychosis has reduced her to gibberish ("'Hi-yip!'") and uncontrollable urination. Here Golding shows the art of concealing an art by bringing the past around full-circle to impinge ironically on the present. Had the earlier portions of the novel been constructed along such invisible lines, they would have been less transparent. The scaffold that was so magnificently dispensable in *Pincher Martin* has become an all too evident excrescence in *Free Fall*.

There are two vital episodes—the interrogation by Dr. Halde and the ending—that lack conviction: the first because it is stereotyped and the second because it is anti-climactic. Inasmuch as Sammy knew of a planned escape from the concentration camp, he is brought before Dr. Halde, a former psychologist turned Nazi, for cross-examination.

Halde is thoroughly aware of Sammy's nature, and particularly of his complete lack of commitment and his artistic sensitivity; he has also accurately gauged Sammy's breaking point and proceeds to rivet away at his resistance with the intensity of a triphammer. Halde, the typical humanist turned totalitarian, can abhor the ruthlessness of his present occupation and rationalize it away as expedient. The reader may feel a certain familiarity with the character of Halde, and he will be right. For Dr. Halde has appeared before in countless disguises as the articulate, dispassionate Gestapo in that host of "B" movies that Hollywood was happily grinding out during World War II. The episode, which could have been a horrifying confrontation between evil and apathy, sinks into a melodramatic interrogation familiar to all movie fans and complete with the inevitable "Bloody swine."

Sammy is then put into a cell where subtle mental torture is applied. He is in complete darkness and alone except for a piece of cold flesh that lies obscenely on the prison floor. The exact nature of the flesh is never specified, but it may very well have been genital;[3] thus Sammy's fears are even more intensified at the prospect of castration. The "center" of his world, to use one of Golding's favorite words, was clearly anatomically limited.

Again, Golding vacillates between the obvious and the artistic. While the Halde episode was shopworn, there is a vigor and originality in the prison sequence that embraces two chapters. The author is in full possession of his powers when he is describing Sammy's mental anguish with the same meticulous care that he lavished on Pincher Martin's ebbing rationalism. But the art wanes with Chapter 8 that begins "How did I come to be so frightened of the dark?" and sees the forging of the all too inevitable link between present and past. Sammy's fears began after his mother's death and his adoption by Father Watts-Watt, whose pitiful advances occasion a digression on misdirected affection. As a child, Sammy fought imaginary enemies in the dark; now he contends with real ones in his prison cell.

It is clear from the beginning of Chapter 10 that Sammy was finally released from the cell, and the rest of the novel concerns his post-war activities. Consequently, if the ending is a gimmick or a re-thinking of the novel, it fails to produce anything comparable to the impact of the final chapter of *Pincher Martin*. The reader is back in the darkened cell; the door opens and a sympathetic officer apologizes for the treatment. Sammy is released with the commandant's feeble explanation, " 'The Herr Doctor does not know about peoples.' " If the final line is supposed to throw the meaning of the novel in high relief (as was the case in *Pincher Martin*), then it is little more than a restatement. The officer's words, while grammatically incorrect, highlight Dr. Halde's totalitarian conception of man: he may know the individual with clinical perception, but he is woefully ignorant of humanity. But this insight would be gratuitous in the light of the interrogation episode which had established the type of person Halde was.

If Sammy's last recollection is of mercy offered in grammatically incorrect terms, then it is anti-climactic. If Sammy is left with one final memory of a beneficent Nazi, then the novel ends optimistically enough (for both Sammy and humanity) but with the banal conclusion that there were some good Nazis. One presumes that the arrangement of the incidents in Sammy's life has the sanction of the author; therefore, the final recollection must coincide with Golding's intentions. But, unfortunately, the ending follows close on the most significant episode in the novel—Sammy's visit to his "spiritual parents," Nick Shales and Rowena Pringle. He has prepared set speeches for each. He would explain Nick's atheism as resulting from the primitive view of God as grim-faced totem. He would show Miss Pringle that her warped view of religion that had no place for the human infected him and, combined with his fallen nature, was responsible for Beatrice's insanity. Regardless, he would offer forgiveness and hope to receive it in turn. But Sammy finds Nick dying in a hospital, and Miss Pringle, overjoyed to see her former student, hopes that she was in some way responsible for his success as an artist.

Both Nick and Miss Pringle represent extremes of which Sammy is aware: "Her world was real, both worlds are real. There is no bridge" (253). Man, then, is in a state of free fall, suspended between a humanism without God and a religion without man. He is like iron filings between two equally strong magnetic poles. Golding is again working from a polarity—religion versus science. It would be futile to expect the author to resolve the dilemma, especially since it seems to be a personal concern.

What is important is that Sammy realizes the existence of a polarity, particularly that both worlds are real and cannot be ignored: "Both worlds exist side by side. They meet in me" (244). Self-knowledge is all that one can ask from memory therapy, and Sammy's introspection has produced a vital realization. Awareness is the first step toward rehabilitation; whether or not it will aid in bringing about a spiritual renovation in a "burning amateur" is another matter. All one can say is that the process has been set in motion. But amateurs do not become professionals overnight.

III A Dark Wood

Another defect in the novel is a symbology that is undeveloped and remains, at best, a blurred blueprint. Golding starts with an interesting premise: a man in his early thirties attempts to review his past life in an effort to see when he fell from grace. A parallel with Dante immediately suggests itself and, for a while, the reader thinks that the theme will be developed along the lines of anti-myth. The narrator is Sammy *Mountjoy*, the surname containing a definite double entendre. He is Sammy *Mons Veneris* ("Mount of Pleasure") and appropriately enough lives on Paradise Hill; his world, it will soon be discovered, emanates solely from the hub of pleasure. Dante first saw Beatrice clothed in red, the patrician color, when both were nine. Sammy meets his Beatrice when their bicycles come to a halt at a red light; both are nineteen. Whereas Dante's Beatrice was the ordering center of his cosmos, Beatrice Ifor is only an instrument for the satisfaction of Sammy's lust. But the parallels soon end; the Dantesque fragments are designed to show what Sammy is not.

It is very easy for the critic to refashion a work and suggest what the author might have done with his material. But Golding is not a novice, and the dictatorial critic would only risk hybris. In *Free Fall,* Golding has abandoned myth for Existentialist soul-baring. One would have preferred (and again this may be hybristic) a mythic development along the lines of a modern *Divine Comedy.* Here Golding would have been in his métier, with a universally recognizable framework arching over the fragmentary memories and spiritual quest of a post World War II wastelander. Instead, he has taken a man whose existence was patternless and proceeded to impose patterns on him.

Although Sammy is the narrator, one feels that Golding's omniscient voice does not quite synchronize with his protagonist's and is usually a bit louder than it should be. It is almost as if he were telling the reader: "Here is a man without any moral direction, but whose past is one large web of connections with the threads carefully aligned in groups of two and producing a dazzling configuration of cosmic chaos." Perhaps the patterns in Sammy's life are really an ironic commentary on his spiritual amorphousness. One would then be led to the heresy of justifying any literary incongruity as irony.

The striking ordinariness of most of Sammy's life does not justify the amount of attention lavished on it. Moreover, when the reader reaches Chapter 12 and meets Nick Shales and Rowena Pringle, the painstaking autobiography and the search for the lost moment of freedom are suddenly eclipsed by a third motif, the two cultures. It appears as if from nowhere and dominates the chapter. This, one suddenly feels, is the novel's burning theme and has very little to do with either Sammy's childhood in Rotten

Row or his deliberate violation of Beatrice. His problem now takes on a desperate urgency. Sammy's inability to bridge the two worlds of science and humanism is part of an eternal debate that had its origin in antiquity with the *nomos-physis* controversy and has found equally vocal support today with C. P. Snow and F. R. Leavis. It is also a question that Golding himself has deeply pondered, for he is acutely aware of what C. P. Snow calls the "gulf of mutual incomprehension" that separates the scientist from the humanist, causing each to dislike and distrust the other.

Golding's career was to have been a scientific one, but he was unable to reconcile science with his literary interests. He is still haunted by the dichotomy between the two cultures. On the one hand, he inveighs against the inordinate position accorded to science: "But it cannot be said often enough or loudly enough that 'Science' is not the most important thing. Philosophy is more important . . . ; so is history; so is courtesy, come to that, so is aesthetic perception." [4] Yet he recently told one critic that after his self-imposed exile from the present: " 'now I must get in some sort of touch with the contemporary scene, and not necessarily the literary one; the scientific one perhaps.' " [5]

Unfortunately, the one problem Sammy has that is not completely self-regarding is never fully developed. Certainly the chapters in which he recalls his religion class with Miss Pringle and his return with explanations and forgiveness are among the finest Golding has ever written; they are also self-contained vignettes which form a miniature novel in themselves. Yet somehow one cannot help feeling that latent in these chapters is the polarity that Golding originally wished to fictionalize. But, like his hero, the author too became immersed in a sea of aimless reminiscence.

There is one final consideration: Sammy is constantly haunted by the loss of his freedom. He claims at the very outset of the novel that he was free as a child and, when confronted by two paths, was able to take whichever he wanted. He was almost, but not entirely free, when he first saw Beatrice Ifor. At first one may think that Golding is equating freedom with innocence, and to some extent he is. Innocence is lost when the virginal mind has its first glimpse into evil (Ralph, Lok). But innocence is a poetic construct like Arcadia or the Golden Age; its loss is inevitable in the maturing process, and one should really speak of the "myth of the loss of innocence" since it is difficult to posit a point in time when it leaves us. Since we cannot recall our childhood innocence, we tend to idealize it.

The loss of freedom is linked with the loss of innocence: to be free is to be able to choose; and, as Golding has said, such an election is the prerogative of the child. It is an experience that only a child knows best; for to the child everything has its own special quality. Odors are particular ones, and each new experience is unique. The appetite has not become jaded. Thus, Golding can speak of freedom as something to be tasted, like potatoes—a simile that is repeated and apparently has some special meaning for the author.

To understand what Golding means by freedom is to accept a paradox. The child is free, but is really unable to lose freedom because he is innocent. As the child matures and passes from innocence to experience, his freedom of choice is naturally hampered by his new-found knowledge. Choice is not quite so simple a thing as which path to take in a park. Still, freedom is not completely lost.

On his graduation day, Sammy considers what he wants most. He hears his own confession:

What is important to you?
"Beatrice Ifor."
. . . .
"If I want something enough I can always get it provided I am willing to make the appropriate sacrifice."
What will you sacrifice?
"Everything" (236).

By deliberately subordinating everything else to his quest for Beatrice, Sammy lost his freedom. There is no longer any choice because there are no alternatives. All that remains is the one overriding goal, the seduction of Beatrice.

Golding's concept of freedom is a theological improvement over innocence, but is still not completely satisfying. To lament innocence is to deplore progress; we believe in our childhood innocence because we cannot remember it. Likewise, to be free is never to use another for personal gratification. This view at least does not beg the question; it simply states the premise on which every Eden is founded. It seems that Golding has written an appendix to *The Inheritors.*

One wishes that Golding had cast *Free Fall* in a mythic mould and filled out the Dantesque outline that was implicit from the beginning. Then it would be able to stand among the great introspective novels of Kafka, Sartre, and Camus. Golding could never have written *Nausea* nor Sartre *Lord of the Flies;* but, in relinquishing the realm of myth in favor of a modern world that at the time was repellent to him, Golding unwittingly trespassed upon Existentialist territory. Simply put, Sartre did it much better in *Nausea.*

CHAPTER 7

The Unsearchable Dispose

"Round about the year 1200, Bishop Poore was standing on a hill over-looking the confluence of the local rivers, according to legend, when the mother of Jesus appeared to him, told him to shoot an arrow and build her a church where the arrow fell. The arrow flew more than a mile and fell in the middle of a swamp. There, with complete indiffer-ence to such things as health, foundations, access and general practi-cability, the cathedral was built. Eighty years later . . . the builders erected the highest spire in the country on top of it, thousands of tons of lead and iron and wood and stone. Yet the whole building still stands. It leans. It totters. It bends. But it still stands. . . ."
—WILLIAM GOLDING, "An Affection for Cathedrals"

I T was inevitable that the blueprint for tragedy that Golding had been tracing in his first four novels should finally be real-ized in the full-scale study of the rise and fall of a man, specifi-cally Dean Jocelin in *The Spire* (1964). In this novel Golding has taken the general framework of a Classical tragedy—someone be-tween the extremes of virtue and vice pursues one goal to the exclusion of all others, thus setting off a complex of events that may result in a dubious triumph but only at the expense of human life—and placed within it the story of Jocelin, Dean of the Cathe-dral of the Virgin Mary, who is obsessed with the vision of cap-ping his church with a spire. His master builder warns him that the foundations cannot support the weight, but Jocelin pays no heed and proceeds with a plan that brings death, madness, but an eventual triumph. For, as Jocelin lies dying, the spire is still stand-ing

The Spire is not only as close a reproduction of Classical tragedy as a contemporary author is likely to achieve, but it is also as transparent an example of myth making as students of literature are likely to find. Golding's Classical allegiance makes his art difficult to define, because it is, like that of the Greek tragedians, the artistic balance of opposites. Each of the tragedians worked with myth that still contained primeval elements—blood guilt, patricide, cannibalism—in short, vestiges of the barbaric past. Each purified the material of its barbarous elements by imposing form on the untempered myth, yet the essential meaning of the tale was unaltered. The tragedians, then, were myth makers in the modern sense of the word, for they created a personal world in which the old and primeval was transmuted into the new and civilized.

Sophocles' *Oedipus the King* is perhaps the ideal example; the tale of Oedipus, involving as it does material of patricide and incest, would have been foreign to a fifth century B.C. audience in its original, unpoetic state. Likewise, Oedipus' cultivated rationalism and the Sophoclean irony, particularly such devices as the violent punning of *oida* ("I know") with the hero's name, would have been equally alien to the early mythographers. The process, then, is the assimilation of myth into dramatic form, just as it would later be of *fabliau* into tale, or chronicle into tragedy. The myth supplies the necessary plot, and the form tempers the primitiveness of the myth.

All of Golding's novels are in some way derivative: *Lord of the Flies* and *The Inheritors* are "parodies" (in the author's sense of the word) of Ballantyne and Wells; *Pincher Martin,* of the Prometheus myth; and *Free Fall,* of Dante with strong confessional overtones. This device is essentially Classical (or traditional in T. S. Eliot's way of thinking) and would seem unoriginal only if the sources have not been thoroughly assimilated and concealed by an overlay of creativity. In *The Spire,* Golding is using the same methods employed by the ancient tragedians: just as they worked from mythical prehistory, he draws on early English history, specifically the construction of the spire of Salisbury Cathedral in the fourteenth century.

Golding has spent much of his life in and around Salisbury, the site of the Cathedral Church of the Blessed Virgin Mary, whose great spire is visible from every point in the city and seems to be pinioning the sky in an act of self-transcendence. Ten miles to the north is Stonehenge, sown with relics of the past including a temple dating from about 1800 B.C.; thirty-five miles away is Avebury and a much larger ancient sanctuary. Wiltshire and the district around Salisbury, an area that Golding knows intimately and loves with a passion that is nationalistic, shows an almost perfect fusion of paganism and Christianity. But, although Christianity succeeded in absorbing a pagan culture, it could no more alter a natural landscape that was wild and windswept than the art of the Greek dramatist could catharize the violent passions of the myths. There is still something defiantly unbaptized about the hills around Salisbury.

Like its setting, *The Spire* is also filled with a tension between the primitive past and the supposedly redeemed present; the author has used the stark framework of Classical tragedy to convey a philosophy of causality that is at once orthodox, inexorable, paradoxical, yet profoundly Christian. But Golding, both moralist and myth maker, draws on fact and shapes it to his own end. Certainly much of what is said in the novel can be corroborated. Jocelin's spire is to have a height of four hundred feet, approximately that of the Salisbury spire. Both are octagonal in shape, and neither was constructed without much rebellion, dissension, and a general indifference to liturgical functions.[1] In 1762 when the capstone of the spire was undergoing repair, a small leaden box containing a relic of the Virgin Mary was discovered in a cavity. In the novel, Jocelin performs one last desperate act of faith by driving a Holy Nail, which had come from Rome, into the very point of the spire.

Moreover, Bishop Poore supposedly received his instructions for building the cathedral in an apparition of the Virgin; Jocelin's inspiration for the spire comes from a vision. According to the guide books, Salisbury is built on marsh land without sufficient foundation to support a structure of this weight; yet the spire stands, as it has stood for six hundred years, and is said to be "built on faith." Both Richard Fairleigh, the architect of the Salisbury spire, and Roger Mason, the master builder of the novel, knew how shaky the foundations were but went ahead with the construction.

But at this point the parallels end. The myth maker uses only so much factual knowledge, and then only as a point of departure for his creative imagination. It is evident that the spire in question is that of the Salisbury cathedral, and the coincidence of certain details easily establishes this point. But there is no evidence in any of the chronicles that the spire was erected at the cost of human life (although it probably was), except in the myth maker's mind. He sees the spire not as an architectural fact but as a symbol that rises toward God from an uncertain foundation, a symbol that compels by its beauty but terrifies by its instability. But the spire is the crowning achievement of a cathedral; it is, in fact, an act of prayer. To the artist who sees in such a construction the seeds of tragedy, there is a more significant question: how can something be designed for God's glory when it threatens human life? Does the raising of a spire, born of a neurotic's vision, warrant the sacrifice of four people? Germs of tragedy latent in the construction of the Salisbury spire elude the literal eye of the chronicler but seize upon the imagination of the artist. The events may never have occurred as Golding describes them; but in art things happen the way they *should* happen. History depicts the particular; but tragedy, the universal.

I *The Tragic Process*

At the core of ancient drama there is always polarity resulting from the tension between the primitive and the civilized, the irrational and the rational; and the tragedian's art brings these contending forces into coalescence. However, there is another type of polarity inherent in the myth itself, and is nothing more than the perennial conflict of opposites. Consequently, one finds the rationalism of Oedipus pitted against the mysticism of Teiresias (*Oedipus the King*), the instinctive barbarism of Medea contrasted with the premeditated sophistry of Jason (Euripides' *Medea*), Antigone's moral law challenged by Creon's man-made edict

(Sophocles' *Antigone*), the frenzy of the Bacchants running counter to the rigid moralism of Pentheus (*Bacchae*). In perpetuating the spirit of Greek tragedy, Golding has inherited this tradition of polarity or tension in the myth.

In *The Spire*, the polarity also determines the structure, for the central conflict—Jocelin's supposedly noble vision to glorify the cathedral despite the dark forces within him that crave expression in the erection of the spire—is the axis around which the novel rotates. The reason for its construction is given at the outset: "They don't know . . . they can't know until I tell them of my vision!" (4).[2] But it is soon made clear that the spire is as much a projection of Jocelin's inner self as it is an external action. One should note, in this respect, the blueprint as Jocelin's sensual imagination has drafted it:

The model was like a man lying on his back. The nave was his legs placed together, the transepts on either side were his arms outspread. The choir was his body; and the Lady Chapel, where now the services would be held, was his head. And now also, springing, projecting, bursting, erupting from the heart of the building, there was its crown and majesty, the new spire (4).

The model, then, is completely physical, with the phallic spire towering over the rest of the members. At the very beginning there is a disproportion in the model that suggests an imbalance in the maker. The spire should exist as the ultimate, crowning glory of a cathedral. Instead, it is the part that will overwhelm the spectator, compelling him to focus attention on only one aspect of the whole.

The spire becomes so bound up with the narrative that the two cannot be separated. This unity is again part of Golding's technique, for one cannot regard the spire as a symbol without seeing its connection with every episode of the novel. Thus the characters exist only insofar as the spire does. Jocelin's obsession reaches the point where everything unconnected with the spire is discarded; man and vision continue to coincide until they are inseparable, until "he understood that all small things had been put on one side for him, business, prayer, confession, so that now there was a kind of necessary marriage; Jocelin, and the spire" (88).

As the fusion of Jocelin and his mission continues, there is a marked personality change. He was first seen transfigured with joy, "God the Father . . . exploding in his face" (3). But a transformation soon occurs. The vision that is really a commitment to excess swells into an obsession, altering everything that comes within its reach. For the construction to take place, religious services in the cathedral are suspended and the high altar barricaded. Devotion is impossible in the midst of scaffolds and workmen who are later revealed to be little more than degenerates. Then Jocelin symbolically steps on the toes of his sacrist, literally depriving him of his livelihood which was earned mostly through the sale of candles. Next there is his indifference to the faithful Pangall, whose impotence makes him a figurehead for the taunts of the workers. To his troubles, Jocelin's dispassionate reply is " 'You're too thin-skinned, man. You must put up with it' " (15).

As the spire ceases to be a form of spiritual adornment and becomes instead a personal obsession, Jocelin views human beings only in terms of the construction and what they can contribute to completion of the spire. He envisions Roger Mason and Goody Pangall enclosed in a tent and separated from the others in exactly the same way as the altar was barricaded from the rest of the cathedral by wood and canvas. The two couples, Roger and Rachel Mason, Pangall and Goody, appear "like four pillars at the crossways of the building" (57). To Jocelin, Roger, his master builder, is an animal in his "open trap" (81), a "prisoner for this duty" (83), a "slave for the work" (84).

Although Jocelin is at first repulsed by Roger's growing attraction to Pangall's wife, he is aware of the practical function that Goody will serve: " 'She will keep him here' " (59). Likewise, Jocelin's need to retain his master builder becomes so intense that he deceives a competitor, thereby causing Roger to lose a better offer. People are measured solely by their usefulness: "If they are part of the cost, why so be it" (95). A series of prodigies consist-

ing of the inexplicable crying of children, the eerie singing of the
cathedral pillars, a plague rumor, an earth tremor, and a raven
that on three separate occasions flies past Jocelin all portend
disaster. But they are unheeded, and the final proof that the spire
has become a personal identification occurs when Jocelin affixes
his own seal to a document to approve additional building costs.

Although Jocelin engages at times in nightmarish fantasies, he
often speaks with the precision of one who fully realizes his position in the cosmic scheme of things. In his speech to Roger Mason,
he makes it quite clear that he knows the role he will play in the
execution of the divine will: " 'When such a work is ordained, it is
put into the mind of a, of a man. That's a terrible thing. I'm only
learning now, how terrible it is. It's a refiner's fire. . . . You and I
were chosen to do this thing together. It's a great glory. I see now
it'll destroy us of course. What are we, after all?' " (83). And
again: " 'You're not in my net—oh yes, Roger, I understand a
number of things, how you are drawn, and twisted, and tor-
mented—but it isn't my net. It's His. We can neither of us avoid
this work' " (115). Thus Jocelin is aware that he is the human
instrument in a divinely established pattern, a link in a chain of
causality that had its origin in eternity. He also knows that, with
the erection of the spire, his role will be over.

But this is Jocelin on the conscious level. Essentially, he is a
modern hero (or anti-hero from the Classical standpoint) whose
soul is in a state of cleavage. Part of it seeks self-transcendence
through an act of faith; part yields to a sensuous reverie with the
slightest provocation: Goody's red hair or the phallic model of a
spire. Jocelin's spirit may look homeward to heaven, but his flesh
is decidedly weak. He is the hero of the divided soul, like Aschen-
bach in Thomas Mann's *Death in Venice,* whose mind vacillates
between the phantasmagoric and the pragmatic. Thus, while
there are times when Jocelin speaks articulately about his role in
the erection of the spire, there are other times when the narrative
becomes halting and ambiguous, streaked with allusions which
the reader must clarify for himself. One must view these passages
—such as the early intimations of a romance between Goody Pan-

gall and Roger, or the deathbed scene when Rachel is presumably speaking of her husband's unsuccessful suicide attempt—through Jocelin's burning delirium.

The tragic process that began in a sunburst of joy ends with the twin paradox of triumph and destruction. The hero achieves the goal he had so relentlessly pursued but, with its attainment, comes his destruction. But, despite the disruption of a community, the disintegration of two marriages, and the deaths of a workman, Goody Pangall, and finally Jocelin himself, the spire still remains. Jocelin has seen his cathedral capped by the spire, which, since the model is the Salisbury Cathedral Church of the Blessed Virgin Mary, will continue to endure as an architectural miracle.

Jocelin also acquires a form of knowledge that eludes most men and that only biblical and tragic figures experience: *"There is no innocent work"* (214). The hero, although broken and divested of his robes, realizes that he has been a minister in the execution of the *opus Dei;* this knowledge is the most awesome type and is denied to ordinary men. But Jocelin is no ordinary man, no more so than Job, Oedipus, and Lear were. He has built an act of faith from human lives; he has experienced the full measure of the proverb, *On ne saurait faire une omelette sans casser des oeufs* ("You can't make omelets without breaking eggs").

Jocelin's final thought on his deathbed is: *"It's like the apple tree!"* (215). Golding has italicized the sentence because it crystallizes Jocelin's total vision in a simile. He had previously described his vision as starting in a simple way, like a single green shoot that first burgeons into tendrils and finally branches. When Jocelin sees an apple tree, the vision takes on an even clearer aspect:

There was a cloud of angels flashing in the sunlight, they were pink and gold and white; and they were uttering this sweet scent for joy of the light and the air. They brought with them a scatter of clear leaves, and among the leaves a long, black springing thing. His head swam with the angels, and suddenly he understood there was more to the apple tree than one branch. It was there beyond the wall, bursting up with cloud and scatter, laying hold of the earth and the air, a fountain,

a marvel, an apple tree; and this made him weep in a childish way so
that he could not tell whether he was glad or sorry (196).

The seeds that were originally planted in earth yield something
that rises above the earth, embracing with its branches whatever
it can enfold; but the tree always rises higher, ultimately toward
heaven.

"*God knows where God may be*" (214). God has chosen Jocelin, whose mind bursts with fantasies as tuberculosis eats away his
spine, to do His work; for, at the end of the novel, the spire is a
finely chiseled monument with its lines rising to a prayer—a bea-
con of spiritual strength for coming generations.

Jocelin has been taken through the same tragic process that
Sophocles devised for King Oedipus. Golding's methods are essentially those of a tragedian, and a comparison with a Greek play,
specifically with *Oedipus the King* (which Aristotle regarded as
the perfect example of ancient tragedy) throws some light on a
novel which is often misinterpreted as just another example of the
author's Calvinism.

1. *A basic polarity consisting of the subtle by-play of conscious
motivation and subconscious desire:* The spire originally conceived as an adornment for a house of God becomes an outlet for
Jocelin's repressed sexuality. Oedipus' highly rational endeavors to
find the murderer of Laius run parallel to, and ultimately coincide
with, his own subconscious attempts to uncover his origins. The
erection of the spire is as much an object of Jocelin's personal
gratification and reverie as Oedipus' investigation is an extension
of his own rationalism.

2. *Fusion of hero and mission.* Jocelin engages in a "necessary
marriage" with his vision. Oedipus' identification with his mission
occurs almost immediately after he hears the oracle's reply, that
the defilement must be expelled from the city. After openly pro-
claiming that he will champion the dead king as if he were his
son, his identification with his cause grows until he has not only
merged with his quest; but, in being the murderer himself, he
becomes the object of the undertaking.

3. *Change in the personality of the king-figure.* Jocelin subordinates everyone and everything to his mission; he allows an adultery that results in Goody Pangall's death in childbirth, drives his master builder to an unsuccessful suicide attempt, turns the cathedral into a home for fornicators and sodomites. Oedipus, who originally regarded himself as a father-king bound by a cosmic sympathy to his children-subjects, evolves into a tyrant. His insistence on clarity becomes a nagging literalism, and thus he taunts Teiresias whose veiled language exasperates him. He even directs his wrath against Creon and finally Jocasta, who, he suspects, is afraid that the investigation will prove him illegitimate.

4. *Tragic knowledge.* In *Oedipus the King,* the final stage in the tragic process is the protagonist's realization that his purpose has been accomplished, but with an ironic and unanticipated outcome. Oedipus' mission has been realized; he has found the murderer of Laius, and in passing from ignorance to knowledge has succeeded in his quest. But the knowledge Oedipus acquires is not merely factual, for the facts themselves are part of a fabric that is Oedipus' own life. In learning about his past, he has learned about himself. Ironically, he has constructed his own biography in which the person investigating coincided perfectly with the object investigated. The end of suffering is knowledge, and in Oedipus' case it was a knowledge that was both personal and universal. Jocelin reaches a similar self-knowledge, but his occurs not at the end of the tragic process but almost at the beginning. He knows the role he will play in this Jobian drama, and he also understands that, with the final curtain, his part will be finished. What Oedipus learned at the end, Jocelin knew at the beginning.

5. *Tragic hero as scapegoat in the working out of the divine will.* Both experience the cycle of *agon* (Oedipus-Teiresias, Jocelin-Roger Mason); *pathos,* or suffering of the scapegoat; and *sparagmos,* or destruction. Neither Jocelin nor Oedipus is spared physical suffering in addition to the inevitable mental turmoil: Oedipus blinds himself, and Jocelin has tuberculosis of the spine. Yet each achieves tragic stature, and in precisely the same way.

From the purely fatalistic standpoint, Jocelin and Oedipus are both instruments in the execution of a divine plan. But more significantly, on the human level, each performs an action that ultimately goes beyond personal gain and benefits the community at large—hence the tragic paradox of triumph and destruction. As an individual, Oedipus is free to pursue the question of Laius' murder or to drop the matter entirely. As king of Thebes, he has, in effect, no other choice but to bring the matter to its conclusion since he knows that the pestilence will be dispelled only with the detection of the murderer. Jocelin's vision is quite similar. What was originally designed as an adornment became instead a consuming obsession. Still, Jocelin's vision was as real as Oedipus' quest, each being a commitment to excess which in turn sets the inevitable tragic process in motion. Yet at the end of both works, each has, however unwittingly, returned to his original purpose: Oedipus has rid his city of the defilement, and Jocelin has seen his cathedral capped by the spire. Oedipus and Jocelin have both attained tragic stature by self-transcendence; in attempting the impossible, they have achieved it.

CHAPTER 8

Lesser Pomps

"This obsession with writing is as pointless as alcoholism and there's no Authors Anonymous to wean you from the typewriter."
> —WILLIAM GOLDING, "It's a Long Way to Oxyrhynchus"

I *The Radio Plays*

ALL of Golding's novels have been successfully adapted for radio plays on the British Broadcasting Corporation's *Third Programme* (roughly the equivalent of FM in America). There is something about Golding's fiction that lends itself to aural presentation (especially in England where radio is still one of the lively arts): the circumscribed action, the timelessness of theme, and particularly the use of sound to convey an aural sensation for which conventional language would be inadequate. Thus, in the novels Golding often writes what might be called "sound cues"; and one thinks immediately of Pincher Martin's scenario for Nat's murder. In *Free Fall,* the opening of a door described onomatopoetically as "Wub wuff!" (60) conveys a much more vivid sound picture than "The door creaked" or some other such statement.

The radio play, *Break My Heart* (1961), is at times incisive, at other times an ordinary picture of life in the English equivalent of a secondary school.[1] A reading of the play leaves one rather unimpressed and somewhat annoyed at the explosion into melodrama that marks the final scene after a beginning and middle that are decidedly tranquil. A hearing of the play in the form for which it was intended, with voices supplying the proper inflections to otherwise ordinary lines, and music swelling in and then subsiding at the right intervals, gives it the immediacy it requires. It is not a short story, but a radio drama; and this distinction is necessary. One expects art from the former because it has a long history of art. Radio drama rarely reaches sublime heights; the listener can only hope to lose himself in a literate script and be carried along to a dénouement that neither defies nor denigrates human intelligence.

Break My Heart has all the earmarks of Golding's technique. There is no formal presentation of the *dramatis personae;* they are introduced as if the listener had known them for years. The play begins with a number of seemingly disconnected scenes of secondary school life, at first dealing with nothing in particular, except an inept faculty incapable of understanding students; but gradually the focus is on the character of Malcom Smith, who cannot memorize Hamlet's "O that this too too solid flesh" soliloquy. Smith's mental block brings the drama to its climax, and the construction of the events leading to it throws much light on Golding's technique, especially his ability to build a scene by employing the entire spectrum of visual and aural effects.

The aged Pennyfeather is thinking of his students and absentmindedly recites their names: "Anderson, Fulbright, Noakes, Rogers, Pain, Smith. Smith—(pause). Why should I think of Smith? Why should I think of anyone? (yawning) Why should anyone think of anyone? Does he think of me? Does he think at all? I wonder what he's thinking now—" A sound cue calls for "WIND. HEART BEAT IN THE WIND." A group of boys chants derisively: "Smith-y, Smith-y, Smith-y, how's yer Ma Smith-y? How's yer Ma?" Smith is heard muttering in his sleep with the background chanting in shrill counterpoint. The sound cue reads: "Chant continues but FADES INTO BACKGROUND. FOREGROUND, STUMBLING STEPS ON A CARPETED STAIR. GIGGLES."

Smith cannot memorize the soliloquy because it is too reminiscent of his own situation: like Gertrude in *Hamlet,* his mother is also involved in an adulterous relationship with her brother-in-law. In the ironic last scene, his teacher tries to explain the context: "You see, Hamlet feels that his mother is almost committing incest by letting her husband's brother make love to her." But then he adds: "At your age you can't understand a thing like this by the light of nature or through experience." Like Hamlet, Smith can only hold his tongue despite his breaking heart. *Break My Heart* reads like the original outline for *Free Fall* with Malcom Smith as the embryonic Sammy Mountjoy who is scarred by an indelible childhood experience, and with his mother, the slatternly Ma of Rotten Row.

Miss Pulkinhorn, set in a cathedral town not unlike Salisbury and dealing with religious extremism, should be considered in connection with *The Spire. Miss Pulkinhorn* (1960) is a semi-Gothic tale of muted violence with the now familiar surprise ending. It is told by a narrator, later identified as Graham, the organist, who establishes the mood in a voice familiar to all radio listeners, British or American—calculatingly ominous: "Darkness in the cathedral. Gleams, no more, from gold and brass and silver. Puddles of half-light from bulbs swinging sometimes on twenty yards of flex. And the echo!"

Graham recounts his first experience with Miss Pulkinhorn, an implacable opponent of change, who criticizes his unorthodox selection of liturgical music. But she is far more concerned about the disquieting presence of a man who interrupts the services with a "hosannah" and whose only comfort comes from seeing the red tabernacle light that proclaims the presence of the sacrament. Again Golding works from a polarity that takes the form of a perennial antagonism—an unbending orthodoxy that can make no allowance for the visionary, and a mysticism that cannot be subjected to church etiquette. We have seen Miss Pulkinhorn before: she is Ralph or Jack, depending upon whose star is in the ascendant in the eternal conflict; she is Homo sapiens casting a dark shadow on a sinless Eden. Hers is the most deadly form of rationalism—the unproductive, which manifests itself only in prejudice. The man is also a familiar Golding character, one of a long line of Christ figures who suffers intensely but inarticulately, and whose name will soon be enrolled in the author's personal litany of saints.

Apparently Miss Pulkinhorn realizes that the man's sanity

hinges on his conviction that the sacrament is present in the tabernacle. Traditionally, when the sacrament is absent, the sanctuary candle is not lighted. One evening, when the eucharist has been removed for the purpose of a sick call, Miss Pulkinhorn stealthily enters the cathedral and lights the candle. The man, who is late for his evening visitation because he had stopped to give his shirt to a beggar, enters to find the light burning but the tabernacle door open. He also finds Miss Pulkinhorn waiting for him in the darkened cathedral with the news that the tabernacle is empty. He dies of shock and despair, but Miss Pulkinhorn with self-righteous complacency claims that her conscience is perfectly clear. "A week later she was dead."

II *The Short Stories*

Miss Pulkinhorn was a serviceable radio drama, but Golding made the mistake of using the same material for a short story.[2] Miss Pulkinhorn's revenge is so grotesque and personal that it can only be described *ex post facto* by the narrator, since it entails an action which Miss Pulkinhorn performs but which the reader would know only if she recounted it herself.

Exposition is not Golding's forte; he is at his best when he weaves fragments of biography in and out of the narrative (*Pincher Martin*) or presents his characters without formal introduction, demanding that the reader establish the necessary relationships for himself (*The Inheritors*). One does not object to a narrator in a radio play, since the solo voice is a long established tradition in this medium; nor does one object to first-person narration in fiction. But a narrator who must explain both the climax and dénouement of an action in which he did not even participate destroys any horror the story might have, for his words will only have the force of conjecture. From the moment Miss Pulkinhorn enters the cathedral, the revenge is completely her own. A switch to the third person would have been far more conducive to suspense than this undesired intrusion of the narrator. This type of subdued horror tale requires subtlety, and one wishes that Golding had studied Faulkner's "A Rose for Emily."

Golding's other attempts at short fiction, "Envoy Extraordinary" (1956), which might best be termed a novella, "The Anglo-Saxon" (1959), and "Inside a Pyramid" (1966) do not leave any lasting impression. "Envoy Extraordinary" has already been discussed in its dramatized form, *The Brass Butterfly,* which is now respectably anthologized and should win more disciples than will the story on which it was based. In "Envoy Extraordinary," Golding has not yet returned from his retreat into antiquity and his writing has an academic and at times musty quality: Mamillius tosses off fragments of transliterated Greek and launches into choruses of Aeschylus' *Seven against Thebes,* the missile is described as tiresomely as the siege operations in Caesar's *Gallic War,* and the humor is of the lecture-hall variety. In the novella, Euphrosyne has a harelip (shades of Ellie May in Erskine Caldwell's *Tobacco Road?*), and Mamillius does not convert to Christianity as he does in the dramatization.

Despite timeliness and urgency, "The Anglo-Saxon" fails to achieve anything like a total emotional effect. It concerns a semi-literate cattle drover, George Smart, who encounters some American soldiers on a road, argues with them over the right of way, attacks one who he thinks is a sergeant, and is taken to jail and fined five pounds. The fine is paid (and this is the surprise ending) by the soldier George assaulted; he is a Negro whose face, apparently disfigured, is covered with bandages of the same color as his skin. The cattle drover turns away, but "did not understand the hot tides that filled his eyes with water." [3]

The weakness of the story stems from an attempt to impart a heroic dignity to a character whose 650-word vocabulary "hung on hooks" in a "dark cupboard," and who brandishes an ashplant in an act of tribal self-assertion. Like Ralph and Lok, he learns through suffering but cannot articulate his feelings. He can only weep; but, what is more pathetic, his tears are a reflex response to a situation he cannot fully comprehend. Again, there is something unspoken and disquieting about the narrative that engenders pathos but fails to convince. Lok, Ralph, and George encounter evil under the form of basic inhumanity. Lok and Ralph witness external manifestations of man's scarred nature, and George beholds man's scarred face. Each is jolted into a knowledge of evil, but lacks the maturity and intelligence to relate this knowledge to some sort of scheme, however nihilistic it may be. Each can only cry.

"Inside a Pyramid" is a story of reminiscence that has much in common with *Free Fall* and "Miss Pulkinhorn." Oliver, the narrator, returns to his home in Stilbourne where he learns that his former violin teacher, Clara Cecilia Dawlish (affectionately called "Bounce"), had died three years previously. The sight of her name on a tombstone occasions an extended reminiscence of his relationship with her. What began as a man's recollection of an unforgettable character ends with a tortured farewell to a woman who was actually a loveless neurotic, totally lacking in the sensitivity that her profession required. Unlike Sammy Mountjoy of *Free Fall* who returned to his teacher, Miss Pringle, with a message of forgiveness, Oliver can only stare at the tombstone and cry: " 'I never liked you" Never!' " [4] And yet he cannot account for the grief that has come over him.

III   *The Essays*

From 1960 through 1962 Golding was a reviewer for *The Spectator,* and in 1961 his non-fiction made its first American appearance in *Holiday,* a magazine with which he has been closely associated. Some of these book reviews and essays have been collected under the title of *The Hot Gates* (1965), which also includes the previously unpublished title piece. What is so refreshing about the *opuscula* is their utter lack of literary overlay or anything that smacks of the belletristic. Golding is not a "literary" writer in the Proustian or Joycean sense. His innovations in style, if they can be called such, are almost editorial: pruning his language, divesting it of abstraction, working over the words.

The essays fall into three classes: travel pieces, humorous sketches, and philosophical observations. When he recounts a trip which he and his family took through the Dutch waterways, takes the reader on a tour of Stratford-on-Avon, or revels in viewing the

English Channel from his plane window, he is writing respectable magazine prose—and nothing more. The humorous sketches are valuable complements to the traditional charcoal sketch of Golding the bearded moralist, for they betray an impish social commentator who is watching the passing show from an ethical vantage point and making playfully acidulous asides on perennial foibles. In "A Touch of Insomnia," Golding invokes the cankered Muse and satirizes the "doctors, lawyers, junior diplomats, supporting actors, scholars, writers not of best-sellers but of books with *réclame*" who are all off for a holiday at sea.[5]

In two accounts of his experiences while writer-in-residence at Hollins College in Virginia, he writes compassionately of the students awkwardly caught between adolescence and adulthood, recalls an encounter with a Negro groundkeeper that oddly resembles "The Anglo-Saxon," or captures all the clichés that abound in a creative writing class. As for his first impression of the Hollins girls: "Under the trees, along the cemented paths, go the drifts of girls, pathetic and charming, giggling or absorbed, shy of the bearded foreigner behind his plate glass, but courteous to the helplessness of old age." [6] Golding is suspicious of creative writing courses, and with good reason if the one he recalls in *"Gradus ad Parnassum"* is any indication of the type he encountered during his American lecture tour. In such a course students and instructor bandy about terms like "sex image," "super-ego" and "id"; and a sensitive youth is told to recast his poem as a sonnet with questions in the octet and answers in the sestet.[7]

Sometimes the essays provide a personal dimension for the novels. Golding has been described as a writer deeply rooted in the anxieties of our time, as one who has spiraled out of the mushroom cloud, holding a dirt-streaked mirror up to man and catching an appropriately murky reflection. The current view is that he is "a bit punch-drunk from the effects of Belsen and Hiroshima." [8] He decries roseate optimism, yet like Plato believes that man can ascend from his fetters in the cave and reach the sun by an understanding of his own nature. In "Before the Beginning," a review of Grahame Clark's *World Prehistory,* Golding wrote that "we can see the sack of Babylon and the blasting of Hiroshima as one and the same thing, a disease endemic but not incurable." [9]

In his novels, Golding exhibits a certain indifference to the characters, a quality that is often found in Classical literature. Sophocles' reconstruction of Oedipus' past, despite the way in which it is made part of the tragedy, has an aura of alienation about it. One does not feel that Sophocles suffered with Oedipus; rather, it is as if Sophocles recorded with poetic precision Oedipus' last day of glory and his fall from eminence. Golding the novelist shows a similar detachment; even in the case of Lok one is profoundly moved, but not to tears. Golding does not suffer with his characters in the way, for example, that Dostoevski did. But then Classicism entails a submission of heart to mind, and the window from which Golding beholds man does not exactly afford a panoramic view.

But in his personal essays there is a warmth and at times a nostalgia that illuminate his other side; Golding can sit for more than one portrait. The essays are a valuable companion to the novels, for they reveal a world view that encompasses much more than the demonic side of man. In "Billy the Kid" [10] he vividly recaptures his emotions as a sensitive eight-year-old. For some reason (perhaps because it is too self-revealing) "Thinking as a Hobby" is absent from *The Hot Gates*.[11] The essay is primarily a series of recollections of teachers and school experiences. When Golding was at Oxford, he saw Albert Einstein standing on a bridge in Magdalen Deer Park. Neither could speak the other's language. Einstein pointed to a trout and said, "Fisch." Golding answered, "Fish. Ja. Ja." At that moment he would have sacrificed every bit of knowledge he had for facility in speaking German.

One expects a future writer to be more awed by another man of letters than by a scientist, and the respect that Golding bore for Einstein is unique and touching. He still hears the siren call of his first interest, science; and it is not surprising that the echo reverberates in his reminiscences.

CHAPTER 9

Epilogue

"It is in some ways a melancholy thought that I have become a school textbook before I am properly dead and buried. To go on being a schoolmaster so that I should have time to write novels was a tactic I employed in the struggle of life. But life, clever life, has got back at me."

—WILLIAM GOLDING, "Fable"

I *The Growth of a Novelist*

A COMMONPLACE of literary criticism is that no true evaluation of an author can occur while he is alive. At this writing, Golding is still productive; and, if *The Hot Gates* is any indication, he will intersperse his writing of novels with essays that are literate without being overtly literary and historical without being archivistic.

His literary career began with a latent *cause célèbre—Lord of the Flies*—that is thematically the least interesting and structurally the least adventuresome of his novels. Even *Free Fall,* despite its imperfections, is characterized by a certain amount of inventiveness, with its shifting chronology and experiments in emotional recollection. It is unfortunate that Golding's first novel elevated him to the position of a campus favorite, a term he deplores. *Lord of the Flies* was never intended as the heir apparent to *The Catcher in the Rye,* nor was it designed as a classic to be shelved alongside *Moby Dick.*

The initial reviews which greeted the book still remain the definitive ones—cautious, moderately favorable, but no barometer at all to the wave of popular acceptance that was soon to engulf it.

Epilogue

It has occasioned a casebook, an anthology of criticism, a plethora of articles claiming analogues from Freud to *Peter Pan*, and has constituted a chapter in at least one doctoral dissertation. On the campus it was required reading for students in political science, used to illustrate the anti-pastoral, and assigned to Peace Corps volunteers to learn "about the essential conflict between man's individual well being and the rules of society." [1] *Lord of the Flies* has also been hailed as the conservative's answer to *The Catcher in the Rye*.[2] Oddly enough, many students claim a staunch allegiance to both novels, a fact which only proves that at least in the university there is little difference between the ultra-conservative and the extreme liberal.

Curiously, some of the academicians who used the book to introduce their students to serious literature (as if the task were that difficult) have now turned on Golding; they find *Lord of the Flies* nothing but "fool's gold": "What is of primary importance is that Golding has used a delicate subject . . . and that thousands of readers have been used in their turn." [3] In this connection Kenneth Rexroth's opinion is worth noting, if for no other reason than its malevolence:

Like Salinger, Golding is one of those authors schoolteachers say all the young read. It's easy to see how this works out. They say to their classes as they assign *Catcher in the Rye* or *Lord of the Flies*, "You have to read this book. All young people think it's terrific. It expresses the alienation of modern youth." So they did with my daughter. "How do you like *Catcher in the Rye?*" "Not much," she said. Later, "How do you like *Lord of the Flies?*" "I can't read it." Maybe she was just raised right.[4]

Perhaps repeated teaching of the novel suddenly made everyone realize it was not all that profound. Child protagonists, like child actors, can be bores when they imitate adults.

The rise of *Lord of the Flies* from a book which went out of print soon after its American publication in 1955 to a paperback best-seller by 1962 could constitute a sociological study in itself. John Peter's article, the first American essay to take a serious look at Golding, appeared in the *Kenyon Review* in 1957; and the inevitable paperback edition of *Lord of the Flies,* complete with a biographical sketch and an interpretation for the uninitiated, was published two years later. In November, 1961, Golding's nonfiction began making its appearance in *Holiday.* He spent a year as a "rarely resident" writer-in-residence (1961–62) at Hollins College; and he also embarked on an American speaking tour that took him to Harvard, Vassar, Dartmouth, the Choate School, the University of Pennsylvania, and even the *Today* television show where, bleary-eyed, he stoically answered questions about Simon's being a Christ figure.

Regardless of its exploitation, *Lord of the Flies* still remains an impressive first novel, and one would be hard pressed to find as good an initial piece of fiction from any of the post World War II novelists. Iris Murdoch, with whom Golding is often paired as a writer of moral concerns (*The Bell* is an excellent companion piece to *The Spire*), also began her career as a novelist in 1954 with *Under the Net,* an utterly academic exercise that lies somewhere between a picaresque novel and a *Bildungsroman* but is actually neither and that shows little of the results she was later to achieve.

The main fault with *Lord of the Flies* is the author's penchant for oversimplification that comes from teaching the young. What was catechetical in the first novel became cosmic in *The Inheritors.* Golding is again exploring the consequences of the problem of evil by forcing the reader to rethink his traditional ideas about his superior self and his inferior ancestors. In his short story, "The Grizzly Folk," H. G. Wells confidently proclaimed that man cannot penetrate the Neanderthal mind: Golding replies that, on the contrary, one could do so; and he brilliantly proved his point.

Pincher Martin was essentially a new novel for Golding, although it did evidence past techniques, especially the trick ending, and anticipated the inverted chronology of *Free Fall.* But more significantly, the existence of evil was taken as axiomatic. Instead of proving the given, Golding merely explored the state of fallen man—or, in the author's words, a man who has "fallen more than most." In its most basic terms, *Pincher Martin* is a morality play with an anti-hero as protagonist. The theophany at the end is as dramatically valid as Death's appearance at the close of *Everyman*. One must remember that Golding was working Greek and, to some extent, biblical motifs into his novel. Therefore, if *Pincher Martin* is "negative," then so is Greek tragedy and the Old Testament. The novel is a parody (always in Golding's definition) of the Prometheus-Zeus tension, except that in it one finds an anti-hero and an anti-God. Even the most practiced blasphemer never answers the Deity with, "I shit on your heaven!"; and no Supreme Being, despite his abhorrence of a moral vacuum like Christopher Martin, replies with the annihilation of a soul—a problem that should puzzle even the most liberal theologians.

One would like to think of *Free Fall* as the Christian reply to Sartre's *Nausea*, and Sammy Mountjoy as a baptized Roquentin. Unfortunately, Golding acknowledges no debt to Existentialism, although one critic has rightly suggested that the affinity is there and that Golding should acquaint himself with the Existentialist novel.[5] Freedom is as much a burning issue in *Free Fall* as it is in *Nausea* and *The Paths of Freedom,* but Golding is not attempting anything quite so ambitious as a fictionalization of *liberté* and *mauvaise foi.* To him, the loss of freedom comes with a hardening of the will against love and with the creation of a macrocosm inhabited and orbited by the self.

There are many flaws in *Free Fall,* particularly the childhood memories which are stereotyped and irrelevant, and an ending which is really an appendix. Yet despite one's reservations about *Free Fall* as a novel, it does show that Golding has once more broken out of the *cul de sac* that often encases the artist preoccupied with the problem of evil. Sammy's introspection does lead him, at least for the moment, out of the Dantesque dark wood. He does see the point in time when he lost his freedom—the minute he made the Faustian pact with himself for the possession of Beatrice.

Unwittingly, Golding has taken the framework of an Existentialist novel and suffused it with an atmosphere of free will. Expressed in "religious" terms (for Golding has called himself a "religious" man), one is free so long as one does not will evil; for, with the willing of evil, man loses his moral center of gravity and falls aimlessly, like an object in space. Although a good deal in *Free Fall* is unsatisfying, it is refreshing to hear the doctrine of individual responsibility reaffirmed.

Golding's exposition of the problem of evil reaches its maturity in *The Spire*, the most perfect evocation of Classical tragedy in our era. The form may seem alien or even at odds with serious contemporary fiction, for we have seemingly lost sight of the heroic. Jocelin, it is true, is an anti-hero; still he has that sense of mission or quest that characterizes an Oedipus, an Aeneas, or a Don Quixote. There is always a tension between Jocelin, the uneducated sensualist cleric, and Jocelin, the perpetuator of a heroic tradition, who attempts a goal that lies beyond the scope of ordinary man.

Golding again reverts to a stark framework on which he hangs the sparse accoutrements of the novel; it is this unadorned core of perennial truth that gives his fiction its universality and causes critics to suggest analogues and influences. Theoretically, all novels centering around a moral polarity are similar; so, too, are novels that are the reminiscences of a solipsistic narrator. In *The Spire*, Golding has taken a theme familiar enough in Classical tragedy—the hero and his vision—and pared it down until it became an axis plunged through the heart of the novel and drawing the episodes around it. Thus in Jocelin one can see traces of Oedipus, Orestes, Aeneas, or even Solness in Ibsen's *The Master Builder*. Like the Classical hero, Jocelin has a superhuman goal. One thinks for a moment of *The Aeneid* and the hero's divine mission to found a new Troy.

Yet, for such a mission to be realized, many lives must be sacrificed: "So great a task it was to found the Roman race" (*Aeneid* I, 33). Aeneas brings suffering and death wherever he goes, but such is the paradox of the hero who carries out the divine will. Jocelin, too, has a mission, although it is partly a projection of his neurosis. He is not a hero, but the author has framed him within a

[100]

heroic proscenium, and he plays his role magnificently. If suffering has any meaning, it can be assessed only in terms of the end result: a Dean's vision of capping his cathedral with a spire does not differ essentially from a Trojan exile's quest for a new home. Each will entail hardship and death; in the last analysis, there is one moral question: was it worth it?

II *Style and Form*

As a stylist, Golding's strength lies in a Classicism that demands a verbal economy and in a construction that is so taut that plot and character become inseparable. Consequently, his best novels —*The Inheritors, Pincher Martin, The Spire*—have a poetic rhythm that moves fluidly from beginning to end. Chapter divisions are merely concessions to convention; it would be more appropriate to speak of the chapters as stanzas, each of which flows directly from the other to produce a vast tragic poem.

Chapters usually begin without any reference at all to a proper name, often with only a personal pronoun. *The Spire* is an ideal example; only once does a chapter begin with a reference to Jocelin. At other times Golding writes: "When *he* woke at dawn next morning . . ." (Chapter 3); "When *he* came to himself in his room . . ." (Chapter 5); "When *he* returned to the spire . . ." (Chapter 6). If the proper name appears at the end of a chapter, there is no need to repeat it at the beginning of the next. Such repetition would only mar the continuity of action. Golding is not being intentionally ambiguous; he is fictionalizing a moral conflict without allowing anything extraneous to subvert his purpose. One expects that economy of plot and characterization will always prevail in his work.

In *Lord of the Flies,* Golding had difficulty integrating his dialogue with the novel's symbolic design. As much as one admired the children's language (their unrehearsed vulgarities, clipped sentences and naïve logic), it never really meshed with the author's luxurious descriptions of the island, his careful use of color, and particularly his adult point of view against which the actions of the boys were ultimately measured.

But in *The Inheritors,* dialogue posed no problems precisely because Neanderthals do not speak in conventional language. Theme and style worked together to produce a novel that was perfectly realized. Since *Lord of the Flies,* Golding has either used dialogue sparingly or else reduced it to fragmentary scenes and monologues (*Pincher Martin, Free Fall, The Spire*) that became a logical part of the overall structure.

Although it is difficult to categorize Golding's novels, Kingsley Amis has suggested that Golding is the only serious writer currently working within the framework of science fiction.[6] Certainly Golding's work shows some of the features of science fiction: an emphasis on ideas to the exclusion of full-blooded characterization, flashes of dark wit but no real humor, an indifference to the female and sex in general, and the use of isolation as a motif although this is really applicable only to the first three novels. But John Peter would use the term "fable," meaning a narrative that gives the impression of being preceded by the conclusion it is supposed to draw.[7] Golding admitted that *Lord of the Flies* was the working out of a preconceived thesis, and one suspects that the same applies to the other novels, although this does not mean that he foresees his conclusions with the exactness of a clairvoyant. Samuel Hynes would borrow a phrase from scholastic esthetics and call the novels "tropological," meaning that they are formed along moral lines and embody traditional ideas about man and his position in the universe.[8] Then there is the author himself, who prefers the term "myth," defined as "something which comes out from the root of things in the ancient sense of being the key to existence, the whole meaning of life, and experience as a whole." [9]

"Fable" comes closest to being the one technical term to cover the Golding *corpus,* although the others are not to be dismissed; they crystallize one aspect of his art, but not the totality. But René Wellek and Austin Warren have proposed a new definition of fable which would be more applicable to Golding: "an abstraction from the 'raw materials' of fiction (the author's experience, reading, etc.)." [10] In his essays, Golding has told us much about his youth: a fear of darkness which he shares with Sammy Mountjoy and Pincher Martin, the quest for a bridge that would span his father's world and his own, compassion for the prehistoric bones he discovered in a youthful excavation, boyhood readings in Homer and Virgil that gave him a sense of the heroic—all have in some way appeared in his fiction. One can also speak of Golding's work as parody, but in his own highly specialized sense—using something else as a point of departure, but always with the qualifying "it may have been that way then but it's different today." Thus *Lord of the Flies* is a "parody" of *The Coral Island; The Inheritors,* of *The Outline of History* and "The Grizzly Folk"; *Pincher Martin,* of the Prometheus myth; *Free Fall,* of the *Divine Comedy;* and *The Spire,* of *Oedipus the King* or of Classical tragedy in general. Golding's technique also comes very close to what Louis MacNeice described in *Varieties of Parable:* one who embarks on parable literature will go back to the world of his childhood, to his island, his sea, his dreams and nightmares, all of which will furnish him with symbols for his writing. Like MacNeice, Golding has written his own commentary on his art.

III   *Quo Vadit?*

Speculation on the future of a productive artist is always hazardous, especially with someone like Golding who has been alternately lauded and scorned. He is often compared with T. S. Eliot, and the comparison is apt. Neither is a spontaneous artist, but each has produced his share of art. Golding labors over his lines with as much care as one imagines Eliot lavished on his verse. Each is intelligible in himself; but both require an awareness, if not a knowledge of the tradition on which they draw, for a total understanding. What has been described thus far is the technique of the Classicist who synthesizes past and present, who assimilates the work of his predecessors into his own.

Golding has progressed from evil as a blind alley in *Lord of the Flies* to evil in the form of suffering as a necessary condition for good in *The Spire.* There is nothing else to be said about evil after this. The essays show that he realizes human beings do not always cast a dark shadow, and perhaps his future work will mirror man in daylight. Golding has also admitted that his fifteen or twenty year sojourn among the ancient Greeks is at an end; and, while he may return to them on occasion, he is now interested in the contemporary world, especially in science. One suspects that the Classic vein is pretty well exhausted; if Golding remains in an empty mine, his voice will only reverberate in vast but hollow caverns. Perhaps he will take up the theme of the scientist and produce the kind of novel C. P. Snow should, but unfortunately cannot, write—a novel in which men are more than working hypotheses.

Golding has stressed the importance of an "Aeschylean" mentality for the novelist by which he meant the necessity of probing the moral conflict, penetrating into the roots of a character's malaise and refusing to be satisfied with a surface examination. In *The Spire*, Golding has achieved the Aeschylean mentality he would demand of others. But a final question remains: where does one go after becoming Aeschylean?

Notes and References

Chapter One

1. *Faulkner in the University*, ed. Frederick L. Gwynn and Joseph L. Blotner ("Vintage Books"; New York, 1965), p. 4.

2. Bernard F. Dick, " 'The Novelist Is a Displaced Person': An Interview with William Golding," *College English*, XXVI (March, 1965), 480. He is equally nostalgic about his poetry in "Crosses," an essay in *The Hot Gates* (New York, 1966), pp. 26–27.

3. "The Writer in His Age," a reply to a questionnaire, in *London Magazine*, IV (May, 1957), 4.

Chapter Two

1. Douglas A. Davis, "A Conversation with Golding," *The New Republic*, CXLVIII (May 4, 1963), 28.

2. *Ibid.*, 30.

3. "It's a Long Way to Oxyrhynchus," *The Spectator*, CCVII (July 7, 1961), 9.

4. In a 1962 interview, Golding was quoted as saying: "If I really had to adopt literary parentage—I don't see why I should—but if I really had to adopt it, I should name thunderous great names like Euripides, and Sophocles, and perhaps even Herodotus. And I might go so far as to say that I have a profound admiration, illogical as it may sound, for Homer." James Baker, *William Golding: A Critical Study* (New York, 1965), p. xvii.

5. Quotations are from the 1858 edition (London).

6. "The Meaning of It All," *Books and Bookmen*, V (October, 1959), 10. For parallels between Ballantyne and Golding, see Carl Niemeyer, "The Coral Island Revisited," *College English*, XXII (January, 1961), 241–45.

7. Quotations are from the Capricorn paperback edition (New York, 1959).

8. On the butterflies as a spiritual symbol (*psyche* in Greek means "soul" and "butterfly"), see Robert J. White, "Butterfly and Beast in *Lord of the Flies," Modern Fiction Studies*, X (Summer, 1964), 163–170.

9. The best discussion of the Dionysiac religion is found in E. R. Dodds's Introduction to his *Euripides Bacchae*, 2nd ed. (Oxford, 1960), an edition which Golding knows intimately.

10. See E. L. Epstein's note in the *Lord of the Flies* Capricorn paperback, p. 250. Specific studies on the Euripidean influence include Bernard F. Dick's *"Lord of the Flies* and the *Bacchae," The Classical World*, LVII (January, 1964), 145–46; Baker, *op. cit.*, pp. 7–10; White, *op. cit.*, p. 170.

11. "The Meaning of It All," p. 10. Golding calls it a "gimmick," thereby introducing a word that was soon to plague him. His explanation of his technique, however, is quite sensible: "Now, look, I have a view which you haven't got and I would like you to see this from my point of view. Therefore, I must first put it so graphically in my way of thinking that you identify yourself with it, and then at the end I'm going to put you where you are, looking at it from the outside."

12. "Lord of the Campus," *Time*, DXXIX (June 22, 1962), 64.

13. "Fable," *The Hot Gates*, pp. 85–101.

Chapter Three

1. H. G. Wells, *The Outline of History*, one volume edition (Garden City, N.Y., 1929), pp. 69–70.

2. "The Meaning of It All," p. 10.

3. Wayland Young, "Letter from London," *Kenyon Review*, XIX (Summer, 1957), 479.

4. Quotations are from the "Harvest Books" paperback (New York, 1963).

5. *The Hot Gates*, pp. 61–70.

Chapter Four

1. Quotations are from the Capricorn paperback (New York, 1962).

2. There is definitely some debt to H. P. Dorling's novel, *Pincher Martin, O.D.* See Bernard S. Oldsey and Stanley Weintraub, *The Art of William Golding* (New York, 1965), pp. 81–82.

3. In which case one will write vindictive articles like Kenneth Rexroth's in *Atlantic*, CCXV (May, 1965), 96–98.

4. Aeschylus, *Prometheus Bound*, 1043 ff., trans. E. A. Havelock, in

Notes and References

Eight Great Tragedies, ed. Sylvan Barnet, Morton Berman and William Burto ("Mentor Books"; New York, 1957), pp. 51–52.

Chapter Five

1. The text of the play is the one in *The Genius of the Later English Theater*, ed. Sylvan Barnet, Morton Berman and William Burto ("Mentor Books"; New York, 1962), pp.445–505.

Chapter Six

1. Quotations are from the Harcourt, Brace & World paperback ("Harbinger Books"; New York, 1962).

2. A sampling of the reviews is given in the Ian Gregor and Mark Kinkead-Weekes article, "The Strange Case of Mr. Golding and His Critics," *Twentieth Century*, CLXVII (February, 1960), 124–25.

3. *Ibid.*, p. 120.

4. "On the Crest of the Wave," *Times Literary Supplement* (June 17, 1960), 387.

5. Baker, *op. cit.* p. 94, n.5.

Chapter Seven

1. See William Dodsworth, *An Historical Account of the Episcopal See and Cathedral Church of Sarum, or Salisbury* (Salisbury, 1814), p. 153.

2. Quotations are from the Harcourt, Brace & World "Harvest Books" paperback (New York, 1965).

Chapter Eight

1. The radio plays are as yet unpublished and can be obtained only from the Scripts Library of the BBC, London.

2. *Encounter*, XV (August, 1960), 27–32. More accessible in *An Introduction to Literature*, ed. Sylvan Barnet, Morton Berman and William Burto, 2nd ed. (Boston, 1961), pp. 228–36.

3. *The Queen*, CCXV (December 22, 1959), 30.

4. *Esquire*, LXVI (December, 1966), 300.

5. *The Hot Gates*, p. 136.

6. "The Glass Door," *The Hot Gates*, p. 141.

7. *The Hot Gates*, p. 156.

8. Oldsey and Weintraub, p. 173.

9. *The Spectator*, CCVI (May 26, 1961), 768.

10. *The Hot Gates,* pp. 159–65.
11. *Holiday,* XXX (August, 1961), 8, 13.

Chapter Nine

1. *"Lord of the Flies* Goes to College," *The New Republic,* CXLVIII (May 4, 1963), 27.

2. Francis E. Kearns, "Salinger and Golding: Conflict on the Campus," *America,* CVIII (January 26, 1963), 136–39.

3. R. C. Townsend, "Lord of the Flies: Fool's Gold?," *Journal of General Education,* XVI (July, 1964), 160.

4. Kenneth Rexroth, "William Golding," *Atlantic,* CCXV (May, 1965), 96.

5. Baker, *op. cit.,* p. 94, n.5.

6. Kingsley Amis, *New Maps of Hell* (New York, 1960), p. 24.

7. John Peter, "The Fables of William Golding," *Kenyon Review,* XIX (Autumn, 1957), 577–92.

8. Samuel Hynes, *William Golding,* Columbia Essays on Modern Writers, No. 2 (New York and London, 1964), pp. 5–6.

9. "The Meaning of It All," p. 9.

10. René Wellek and Austin Warren, *Theory of Literature* (New York, 1949), p. 226.

Selected Bibliography

Primary Sources

1. Major Works by William Golding

Since all quotations from the novels have been taken from the paperback editions, they are also included in the bibliography as being the most accessible.

Poems. London: Macmillan's Contemporary Poets, 1934.

Lord of the Flies. London: Faber & Faber, 1954; also Capricorn Books; New York: G. P. Putnam's Sons, 1959.

The Inheritors. London: Faber & Faber, 1955; also Harvest Books; New York: Harcourt, Brace & World, 1963.

Pincher Martin. London: Faber & Faber, 1956; also Capricorn Books; New York: G. P. Putnam's Sons, 1962.

"Envoy Extraordinary," in *Sometime, Never: Three Tales of Imagination* by William Golding, John Wyndham and Mervyn Peake. London: Eyre & Spottiswoode, 1956, pp. 11–78.

The Brass Butterfly. London: Faber & Faber, 1958; also in *The Genius of the Later English Theater*, ed. Sylvan Barnet, Morton Berman, William Burto. Mentor Books; New York: The New American Library, 1962, pp. 439–505.

Free Fall. London: Faber & Faber, 1959; also Harbinger Books; New York: Harcourt, Brace & World, 1962.

"The Anglo-Saxon," *The Queen,* CCXV (December 22, 1959), 27–30.

Miss Pulkinhorn. A radio play presented on the BBC April 20, 1960; short story version published in *Encounter*, XV (August, 1960), 27–32; available in *An Introduction to Literature*, ed. Sylvan Barnet, Morton Berman, William Burto. 2nd ed. Boston: Little, Brown & Company, 1961, pp. 228–36.

Break My Heart. A radio play presented on the BBC March 19, 1961. Remains unpublished.

The Spire. London: Faber & Faber, 1964; also Harvest Books; New York: Harcourt, Brace & World, 1965.

The Hot Gates. London: Faber & Faber, 1965; first American edition, New York: Harcourt, Brace & World, 1966.

"Inside a Pyramid," *Esquire,* LXVI (December, 1966), 165, 302.

2. Essays and Reviews by William Golding

Note: Those marked + are included in *The Hot Gates.*

London Magazine, IV (May, 1957), 45–46. A reply to a questionnaire "The Writer in His Age."

"Pincher Martin," *Radio Times,* CXXXVIII (March 21, 1958), 8.

+"The Ladder and the Tree," *The Listener,* LXIII (March 24, 1960), 531–33.

+"On the Crest of the Wave," *Times Literary Supplement* (June 17, 1960), p. 387.

"In Retreat," *The Spectator,* CCIV (March 25, 1960), 448–49. Review of Raleigh Trevelyan's *A Hermit Disclosed.*

"Raider," *The Spectator,* CCIV (May 20, 1960), 741. Review of Samuel Eliot Morison's *John Paul Jones.*

+"Islands," *The Spectator,* CCIV (June 10, 1960), 844–46. Review of *The Swiss Family Robinson* and *Treasure Island.*

+"Headmasters," *The Spectator,* CCV (August 12, 1960), 252–53. Review of T. W. Bamford's *Thomas Arnold.*

+"In My Ark," *The Spectator,* CCV (September 16, 1960), 409. Review of Gavin Maxwell's *The Ring of Bright Water.*

"Man of God," *The Spectator,* CCV (October 7, 1960), 530. Review of Lesley Blanch's *The Sabres of Paradise.*

+"Billy the Kid," *The Spectator,* CCV (November 25, 1960), 808, 811.

"Prospect of Eton," *The Spectator,* CCV (November 25, 1960), 856–57. Review of Christopher Hollis' *Eton.*

"Thin Partitions," *The Spectator,* CCVI (January 13, 1961), 49. Review of Russell Brain's *Some Reflections on Genius and Other Essays.*

"Rise of Love," *The Spectator,* CCVI (February 10, 1961), 194. Review of John Bayley's *The Characters of Love.*

"Androids All," *The Spectator,* CCVI (February 24, 1961), 263–64. Review of Kingsley Amis' *New Maps of Hell.*

"All or Nothing," *The Spectator,* CCVI (March 24, 1961), 410. Review of *The Faithful Thinker,* a collection of essays celebrating the centenary of Rudolf Steiner, ed. A. C. Harwood.

Selected Bibliography

"Before the Beginning," *The Spectator*, CCVI (May 26, 1961), 768. Review of Grahame Clark's *World Prehistory*.

+"Astronaut by Gaslight," *The Spectator*, CCVI (June 9, 1961), 841–42. Review of eight tales by Jules Verne.

"It's a Long Way to Oxyrhynchus," *The Spectator*, CCVII (July 7, 1961), 9.

"Party of One: Thinking as a Hobby," *Holiday*, XXX (August, 1961), 8, 13.

+"Tolstoy's Mountain," *The Spectator*, CCVII (September 8, 1961), 325–26. Review of *War and Peace*.

+"A Touch of Insomnia," *The Spectator*, CCVII (October 27, 1961), 569–71.

+"The Glass Door," *The Spectator*, CCVII (November 24, 1961), 732–33.

+"The English Channel," *Holiday*, XXX (November, 1961), 32, 41.

+"Body and Soul," *The Spectator*, CCVIII (January 19, 1962), 65–66.

"Through the Dutch Waterways," *Holiday*, XXXI (January, 1962), 58 ff.

+"Shakespeare's Birthplace," *Holiday*, XXXI (May, 1962), 82 ff.

+"*Gradus ad Parnassum*," *The Spectator*, CCIX (September 7, 1962), 327–29.

"Surge and Thunder," *The Spectator*, CCIX (September 14, 1962), 370. Review of Robert Fitzgerald's translation of the *Odyssey*.

+"Digging for Pictures," *Holiday*, XXXIII (March, 1963), 86 ff.

"Party of One: The Best of Luck," *Holiday*, XXXV (May, 1964), 12, 17.

"An Affection for Cathedrals," *Holiday*, XXXVI (December, 1965), 35, 42.

Secondary Sources

Articles marked * are included in *William Golding's "Lord of the Flies": A Source Book*, ed. William Nelson. New York: Odyssey Press, 1963. Those marked ** are in *Casebook Edition of William Golding's "Lord of the Flies,"* ed. James R. Baker and Arthur P. Ziegler, Jr. New York: G. P. Putnam's Sons, 1964. It should be noted that *all* articles in the above books are relevant and highly recommended for students.

BAKER, JAMES R. *William Golding: A Critical Study*. New York: St. Martin's Press, 1965. A scholarly, thoroughly readable study by one of Golding's main American exponents, with an especially useful bibliography.

DICK, BERNARD F. " 'The Novelist Is a Displaced Person': An Interview with William Golding," *College English*, XXVI (March, 1965), 480–82. Golding on poetry, Freud, and Greek tragedy.

**EPSTEIN, E. L. "Notes on *Lord of the Flies*," in *Lord of the Flies*. Capricorn Books; New York: G. P. Putnam's Sons, 1959, pp. 249–55. Biographical sketch plus critique including the now famous (?) "Oedipal wedding night" interpretation of the "pig-sticking."

*GINDIN, JAMES. " 'Gimmick' and Metaphor in the Novels of William Golding," *Modern Fiction Studies*, VI (Summer, 1960), 145–52. Reprinted in Gindin's *Postwar British Fiction*. Berkeley: University of California Press, 1962. Claims that the ending in each of the first four novels "palliates the force and unity of the original metaphor." The problem might have been obviated if *deus ex machina* in the Euripidean sense were chosen as a critical term, although Golding himself used the word "gimmick" vis-à-vis his first three novels (*Free Fall*, in his opinion, is not "gimmicked").

*GREEN, PETER. "The World of William Golding," *A Review of English Studies*, I (April, 1960), 62–72. Especially useful for influences and analogues.

*GREGOR, IAN and MARK KINKEAD-WEEKES. "The Strange Case of Mr. Golding and His Critics," *Twentieth Century*, CLXVII (February, 1960), 115–25. A good but too high-powered pitch for *Free Fall*.

HYNES, SAMUEL. *William Golding*. "Columbia Essays on Modern Writers." No. 2. New York and London: Columbia University Press, 1964. A valuable monograph, somewhat nebulous on Golding as fabulist, but quite lucid on *The Spire*.

*KERMODE, FRANK. "The Novels of William Golding," *International Literary Annual*, III (1961), 11–29. Reprinted in Kermode's *Puzzles and Epiphanies*. New York: Chilmark Press, 1962. A sane evaluation by one of Golding's earliest admirers.

———— and WILLIAM GOLDING. "The Meaning of It All," *Books and Bookmen*, V (October, 1959), 9–10. Unscripted discussion broadcast on the BBC. Golding on Ballantyne, Wells, "gimmick," and the damning of Pincher Martin.

MACLURE, MILLAR. "Allegories of Innocence," *The Dalhousie Review*. XL (Summer, 1960), 145–56. Although not exclusively on Golding (it extends also to Faulkner and Camus), this strangely neglected essay takes the most sensible approach to "innocence" as something we do not remember but merely believe.

* **NIEMEYER, CARL. "The Coral Island Revisited," *College English*,

XXII (January, 1961), 241–45. Shows Golding's use of Ballantyne without overstating the case. Significantly, Golding quotes part of this essay in "Fable." (*The Hot Gates,* pp. 88–89).

OLDSEY, BERNARD S. and STANLEY WEINTRAUB. *The Art of William Golding.* New York: Harcourt, Brace & World, 1965. An extremely well-written account by two men who are conversant with Golding's world and literature in general. The Golding *corpus* is put in a literary perspective by a judicious choice of analogies.

* **PETER, JOHN. "The Fables of William Golding," *Kenyon Review,* XIX (Autumn, 1957), 577–92. The first important critical essay on Golding in America (and one which he especially likes); notable for its distinction between "fable" and "fiction."

WHITE, ROBERT J. "Butterfly and Beast in *Lord of the Flies,*" *Modern Fiction Studies,* X (Summer, 1964), 163–70. A symbolic reading hinging on the idea of "butterfly" as a spiritual symbol.

Index

Names of characters in Golding's works are followed by the title—in parentheses—of the book in which they appear.

[115]

Index

Index